TELEVISING WAR

Televising War
From Vietnam to Iraq

Andrew Hoskins

continuum
LONDON • NEW YORK

Continuum International Publishing Group

The Tower Building   15 East 26th Street
11 York Road   New York, NY 10010
London SE1 7NX

British Library Cataloguing-in-Publication Data
A catalogue record for this book is available from the British Library.

ISBN: 08264 7305 9 (hardback)
        08264 7306 7 (paperback)

Typeset by Servis Filmsetting Ltd, Manchester
Printed and bound in Great Britain by The Cromwell Press, Trowbridge, Wiltshire

For my parents

Contents

Acknowledgements

The beginnings of this book benefited greatly from the dynamic research environment of the Department of Sociology at Lancaster, which I was privileged to be a part of for much of the 1990s. I am grateful to John Urry for his interest in my work and for his advice and I am particularly indebted to the late Deirdre Boden who first inspired me to think and write about television and memory.

I am also grateful to Marie Gillespie and James Gow for their insights on news cultures and the Iraq War in conversations leading to our successful application to the ESRC New Security Challenges Research Programme. And I would like to thank Victoria Cook at the Imperial War Museum and Lena Munday for their help in relation to Holocaust memory.

Thanks are also due to Kevin Williams for his encouragement and to Christina Parkinson at Continuum for her support and professionalism.

For their longer term contributions I would like to thank Jonathan Nicholson, Alison Jones, Rob John, Martin Jarvis, William Merrin and Amanda Egner.

Finally, this book would not have been possible without the belief, patience, hard work and good humour of Beth Linklater.

Preface

My memories of the 1991 Gulf War are not very clear, at least not from watching it on television at the time. I do, however, possess a definite memory of the context, notably writing undergraduate essays night after night in a student house with the war unfolding on continuous news coverage on a portable black-and-white TV set in the background. Yet, even with the very real clarity of my remembering of these circumstances today, it is unlikely that the image in my mind is particularly accurate. Human memory, after all, is continuously developed from one's own reflections (and from those of others), whereas my memory of what actually appeared on television in early 1991 is fundamentally different, being of something 'artificial', mediated. Although my own reflections certainly alter what I remember, the Gulf War that has since been remade on television and other media more powerfully reshapes my memory. And this, essentially, is the problem posed in this book.

I came across the television Gulf War when I was introduced to Deirdre Boden at Lancaster University in 1994. On her office shelves were about 80 videotapes containing continuous American TV coverage of the war. She later said that she didn't know quite why she was recording the war at the time but she knew that it was important to do so – to have some sort of record of this television event or, rather, 'experience'. It struck me that these tapes had a completeness about them, containing a chronology, a set, and constituted a 'history'.

This book had its early glimmerings in that particular collection of recordings and in conversations with Deirdre Boden whose insights into television and memory were never published (given her premature death in 2001). She treated television as a medium of people who in various ways *made* history on a moment-to-moment reflexive basis, and to understand the latter, one must begin by detailing the former. Hopefully, there is something of her approach in what follows, and not least in beginning to document the capacity of news correspondents to witness and shape unfolding histories around the media-military images of the 2003 Iraq War.

Obviously, the attempt to make sense of an unfolding media event does not benefit from the reflection and retrospection afforded by the time elapsed since the Gulf War. The term 'media event' is, in fact, slightly misleading, for the dynamics of television news unsettles the past (including through its compulsive repetition). What one aims to do is to identify the continuities and the historical trajectories of events as they are re-visited and re-defined through the prism of the present. The experience of the early twenty-first century, including the Iraq War and September 11, 2001, demonstrates the absolute intersection between the media and its subject matter. And any adequate history of these times will need to recognize and fully implicate the reflexive documenting function of the media in the modern world. The account here attempts to contribute to this emerging history.

Chapter 1

Conflicts of memory in a media age

AN INTRODUCTION TO MEMORY AND MEDIA

I think we're gonna have to remember September 11 in its reality. Much the same way as we have to remember other horrific events in our history. Because somehow I think it pushes the human consciousness toward finding ways to avoiding this in the future. But if you censor it too much, if you try to find too many euphemisms for what happened, then I think you rob people of the ability to actually relive it and therefore motivate them to prevent it from happening in the future.

(Mayor Rudolph Giuliani, In Memoriam New York City,
Channel 4, 4 September 2002)

Mayor Giuliane's reflections on September 11 illustrate important features, functions and conflicts in the nature of 'memory' in modern societies. Giuliane considers that for the city of New York and other Americans to deal with the horrors of the terrorist attacks of September 11, 2001, they need to acknowledge them, rather than allowing them to become merely part of an unspeakable past. Remembering from this perspective involves engaging explicitly with past events rather than allowing them to become part of a superficial memory that is retained only in a façade of the past.

Catastrophic events, as the then mayor of New York implies, can be assimilated into sanitizing language and images that afford a less painful or shocking view (perhaps 'September 11' or '9/11' have become such euphemisms) and produce a more 'manageable' past. That is to say, societies often represent their own past in a form that is acceptable to current generations. Past events that are too painful to tolerate, or are an uncomfortable part of a nation's history, can be retold with the cushion of time that has since elapsed. Inevitably, this involves the reshaping of events over time as they are retold and re-presented with 'forgetting' a necessary part of the fallibility and the selectivity of memory. *Reliving* past events is part of the very essence of memory, be this from within – in the human mind – or via their social articulation – from informal conversation through to public documentation and commemoration. We attempt to manage our own individual memories through suppressing, reshaping and forgetting painful experiences in our past, and bringing to the fore happier past times.

Beyond the individual human mind this process has been variously described as: 'collective memory' (Halbwachs, 1992/1952); 'cultural memory' (Sturken, 1997); and 'social memory' (Reading, 2002), for example. Barbie Zelizer (1998) in her effective analysis of images of the Holocaust in collective memory observes that, 'Unlike personal memory, whose authority fades with time, the authority of collective memories increases as time passes, taking on new complications, nuances, and interests' (p. 3). In this way, the individual is reliant on others, on the collective, to sustain their own memory, as Halbwachs (1992/1952: 39) argues:

> Most of the time, when I remember, it is others who spur me on; their memory comes to the aid of mine and mine relies on theirs. There is no point in seeking where they are preserved in my brain or in some nook in my mind to which I alone have access for they are recalled to me externally, and the groups of which I am a part at any time give me the means to reconstruct them, upon condition to be sure, that I turn toward them and adopt, at least for the moment, their way of thinking.
>
> It is in this sense that there exists a collective memory and social frameworks for memory; it is to the degree that our individual thought places itself in these frameworks and participates in this memory that it is capable of the act of recollection.

Memories do not reside as a 'store' in the mind – as is perhaps our every-day understanding of human memory – but instead are *provoked*, being challenged, altered, sustained and shared by others. Collective memory, in this way, is the product of a negotiation between individuals and their wider surround at a given time and in a given context. Although in this same way, the term collective memory itself seems to imply a more unified and consistent body than perhaps is attainable or identifiable in the shifting relations that constitute what and how we remember. In this way, the term social memory (that I use hereafter) is more appropriate, for it is not bound by the collective, but exists in and beyond the individual and the group and is dynamic within societies and across them. Susan Sontag (2003: 86) for example, states: 'What is called collective memory is not a remembering but a stipulating: that *this* is important, and this is the story about how it happened, with the picture that locks the story in our minds.' Collective memory may thus be an ideal and an aim of societies (and of 'social frameworks') but social memory is their practice.

What has changed is that there appears to be a growing premium placed on individual and social memory in modern societies. *Why* and *how* the past is remembered has increasingly become a source of conflict, particularly over how catastrophic events should be publicly marked and collectively remembered. For instance, forms of remembrance of the deaths of millions (the Holocaust), thousands (September 11), or even one individual (Diana, Princess of Wales) have provoked public and government debate and outrage and have even been subject to judicial process. The motivation often stated for the marking of catastrophes involving human death and suffering is the hope that future generations will 'not forget' and so ensure that such events will not be repeated. The Holocaust is one of the principle subjects of debate over collective memory in the modern world. Jeffrey Shandler (1999: xv), for example, details the means through which 'memory culture' of the Holocaust has developed in Europe and in America:

> In Europe, the former Soviet Union, and Israel, Holocaust remembrance has been realized as powerfully, if not more so, through the presence of survivors of World War II or geographical landmarks. But in America this subject has almost always been mediated through newspapers, magazines, books, theaters, exhibition galleries, concert halls, or radio and television broadcasting.

Here Shandler encapsulates three of the principal components of memory in modern society, namely: people, place, and media. Firstly, those who actually experienced an event or were eyewitnesses to it carry with them literally a living memory. Their accounts are often treated as primary sources by historians and others wishing to learn more about past events. Secondly, the place in which an event has taken place is often attributed special significance, as though by standing in that place one can imagine its history. John Urry identifies spaces which have been designed as sites for spending time, rather than merely 'passing through'; he argues, 'This seems to presuppose a glacial sense of time, to feel the weight of history, of all the memories of *that* place, and to believe that it will still be there in its essence in many generations' time' (1994: 140). Today, place has become even more important to social memory and particularly the site at which people have been injured and killed. The significance attached to Ground Zero in New York, for example, is the very antithesis of the placelessness of the electronic mediation of this event. And it is the role of the mass media as the third principal shaping force of memory in our modern world that is my central concern here.

At the very least the media has encroached upon many of our traditional forms of remembering. The 'balance' of social memory has shifted and is shifting from eyewitness and living memory to more mediated forms of remembering; indeed, the latter has become the principal vehicle of the former. Mayor Giuliani's remarks were made on a television documentary *In Memoriam: New York City*, broadcast to commemorate the lives lost on September 11, 2001. This programme compiles a ubiquitous and also terrifying account using visual and audio footage from 16 news organizations and 118 survivors and onlookers. It functions not only as an instance of commemoration but also as a detailed historical document created from every possible angle: people filmed as they ran (Hoskins, 2004). The capacity of the electronic media (through individuals' use of highly portable and inexpensive equipment) to forge such a visually comprehensive account poses new challenges for social memory.

Visual images are particularly vital to memory, to our orientation to the world 'out there' and to history. Raphael Samuel (1994: 27), for example, argues that, 'The visual provides us with our stock figures, our subliminal points of reference, our unspoken points of address.' The media, as today's principal source of visual images, powerfully shape or direct social memory. Moreover, in circumstances in which the medium of television is the primary 'subliminal point of reference' and is increasingly the 'original' means of production of our experiencing of world events, it makes sense to examine media data and its dissemination in order to help understand the shaping of social memory. What, for instance, would a memory of the attacks on America of September 11, 2001 'look like' without the televisual and photographic images? How would a global memory of this event be forged with only written and spoken eyewitness testimony, and how long would it take for such a memory to be established?

NEW MEMORY

Television and particularly television news produce a new and apparently reliable stream of historical consciousness of today's events. Although human memory appears authentic to one's self, one's biography, and one's identity it is nonetheless unreliable, whereas mediated images and events, although equally selective, are potentially more enduring. The notion that our individual and social memories are increasingly intertwined with and reliant on media data is a problem of *new memory* (Hoskins, 2001b). On the one hand the media powerfully sustain past events through the repetition of key or 'stock' images, whilst on the other, they force upon audiences an amnesia of events not deemed newsworthy.[1]

New memory is forged in an environment saturated by the media. Moreover, contemporary mediated events are marked by their immediacy. The time between the occurrence of an event and its dissemination as news has shrunk, so that often audiences watch events as they unfold live in real-time, implicating themselves in events as vicarious witnesses. Alastair Cooke, for example, in a *Letter from America* in March, 2003, puts these transformations into perspective by citing his own words written 30 years earlier:

In the First World War the statesmen and generals and correspondents waited many years before they told us of the horrors and the scope of the casualties.

Here now in Vietnam young correspondents in sweaty shirts poke microphones into a soldier's face and hear him say he doesn't know what he's there for. There is no gap between the battlefield and the memoirs.

I don't think it's possible to exaggerate the shattering capacity of television to tell it *now* and what is shattered, I suspect, is morale – both at the front and at home. (original emphasis)[2]

Today, these features of reporting war and other events have reached a new intensity. Saturating and extended news coverage provides little relief in terms of the space and distance necessary for memory to become 'settled': television appears as our dominant surround, delaying or disabling the forgetting function of social memory.

The repetitious and saturating media coverage of September 11, for example, delayed new contexts and narratives from being forged, i.e. audiences could not quickly contextualize this event as past whilst being confronted with it in a perpetual present. Instead, a glut of circulating images effected a *collapse* of memory, undermining the natural pace of social memory to both remember and to forget. In this way, television in particular can be said to prevent memory through its satiation and over-load of images, yet at the same time it crystallizes memory of events around scenes it obsesses over, for example: the planes hitting and the collapse of the twin towers of the World Trade Center; the green 'nightscape' view of Baghdad speckled with upward tracer fire at the opening of the 1991 Gulf War; and the publicly-captured knowing embrace of President Clinton and the White House intern, Monica Lewinsky. All these are defining moments in television global history (remediated in print and other media) where images become almost instantaneously iconic through their mass dissemination and repetition. These also come to form media 'flashframes':[3] images seemingly burned into history through their use as visual prompts in news programmes and other media so that they are instantly and widely recognizable as representing a particular event or moment in history. In this way, media flashframes can become static – as fixed forms of representation – and thus not vulnerable to the dynamics and forgetfulness of the human brain.

Steven Rose, for example, in *The Making of Memory* traces the beginning of what he terms 'artificial' memory (as contrasted with 'natural' or human memory). In early human societies, for example, memory was wholly reliant on the oral telling of stories of the past, so that 'What failed to survive in an individual's memory, or in the spoken transmitted culture, died forever' (1993: 60). In modern societies however, Rose argues, artificial memory has a significant influence over what is remembered (and forgotten):

> The new technologies change the nature of the memorial processes. A video or audiotape, a written record, do more than just reinforce memory; they freeze it, and in imposing a fixed, linear sequence upon it, they simultaneously preserve it and prevent it from evolving and transforming itself with time. (1993: 61)

Media flashframes, however, are crucially composed of images or sequences of images: the Zapruder film of the assassination of John F. Kennedy in 1963 (only much later remediated on television); student demonstrations in Tiananmen Square in May 1989; and the Rabin–Arafat handshake facilitated by Clinton on the White House lawn in 1993 – these are all events image-driven into social and global memory via their repetition on television and across other media.

The apparent vividness and immediacy of media flashframes can lead to a mis-remembering of events; people seeing an event revisited on television in later times can easily convince themselves that they witnessed it originally on TV. Deborah Esch (1999), for example, refers to a poll showing that a majority of Americans believed they had witnessed the Kennedy assassination live on television. In actual fact, Esch points out, the original Zapruder film had been stored in a vault at *Time-Life* until five years after the event, and had only been available as photographs during this period.[4] In this way, individual remembering and mis-remembering is shaped by distant media images as perceptually immediate stimuli. Events are re-narrated over time through television whether or not they were originally witnessed in real-time through the same medium. TV functions in a similar way to human memory in repeating and reenacting events, as Marita Sturken (2002: 200) argues,

> television's reenactment is much closer to the fluid ways in which memory operates not as a stable force but as a constantly rewritten script. Renarratization is essential to memory; indeed, it is its defining quality. We remember events by retelling them, rethinking them.

Yet, under the conditions of 'event time' (see Gitlin, 1980) where TV firstly ensures that something happens, and secondly organizes itself around the happening, there occurs a certain *displacement* of anything outside of the event itself.

How though do images become flashframes? Central to the development of new memory is the role of journalists, editors, and other news-workers. Clearly, picture and video editors, in their original as well as repetitive selecting of images, are influential in shaping what is seen and remembered and what is not seen and not remembered. However, it is *journalistic discourses* that illuminate and direct the significance of images and stories that come to frame our understanding of past events. Michael Schudson, for example, in his analysis of the public 'mis-remembering' of the former US President Ronald Reagan, found that an 'oral culture' of political elites and journalists was broadcast via the media and so entered into socially-constructed 'myth': 'There is, we might say, a rhetorical structure to social institutions, a patterned way in which language comes to be used; once used, referred to; and when referred to, remembered and drawn upon as part of what "everyone knows" (1990: 118). Although Schudson is referring here to political journalists, it is clear that news discourse is more widely shaped by the 'personal encounters and oral communication' of journalists (ibid.) whose own collective memory feeds our wider social memory as audiences.

And it is precisely this pool of discourses and images that become recognized and drawn upon as part of what 'everyone knows' that forges social memory through the media. Television news today, for example, has a rolling presence and helps sustain that which Hargreaves and Thomas (2002: 44) define as 'ambient news' – for it is 'like the air we breathe, taken for granted rather than struggled for'. The news 'where you want it, when you want it', for example, is one of the promotional slogans of the BBC News 24, one of the many TV channels providing news all day, every day.

Yet to grasp the phenomenon of new memory requires investigation into *how* these images re-enter individual, social or global consciousness in new times and in new contexts. A key paradox of media flashframes is that their apparent stasis in and over time jars against the idea that memory necessarily involves the representing of a past event in the present, that is in a *new* and *different* moment. These ideas at least in relation to human memory are not new. Psychologists, for example, have for some time drawn upon Bartlett's experiments with memory in relation to time from the 1920s and 1930s. The key process of remembering for Bartlett was the introduction of the past into the present to produce a 'reactivated' site of consciousness (1932; Norman, 1976: 224). The event, image, or time being sought for retrieval is not revived but, rather, recreated in a new present-moment context.

The mass media constitute powerful and extensive sites for the 'reactivation' of past events, and in recent years especially, television has entered into the actual production of the events it records, in that process altering the moment-by-moment trajectory of events (Boden and Hoskins, 1995). Particularly subject to the transformations of new memory are those events subject to the most media attention, and at a global level these mostly concern war and other catastrophes. What follows is an investigation into the new memory of contemporary warfare, notably the 1991 Gulf War and the 2003 Iraq War as defining media events of our age, linked by and through the media and memory. These wars are uniquely connected through the chief protagonists (Saddam Hussein, and the two Presidents Bush). Moreover, both wars shaped and were shaped by critical junctures in the development of global and real-time media, and in relations between the media and the military.

AN ETHICS OF VIEWING

In the last quarter of a century the mass media have helped propagate the myth that warfare (fought by the West at least) can be 'limited', 'surgical', and 'clean'. Despite the accounts and images that have subsequently undermined the 'smart' political and media discourses that characterized the 1991 Gulf War, the latter seem to persist in social memory. It appears that the originally received media flashframes of an event endure despite later contradictory revelations. For example, a divergence has occurred between a revisionist history of the media's responsibility for 'losing' the Vietnam War, and an enduring social memory or myth that continues to overwhelmingly implicate television news coverage in undermining the US military campaign in Vietnam.

Images that depict the shocking realities of warfare and catastrophe are said to be more memorable, because of their initial impact on the viewer. However, the media and audiences treat images of death very differently according to their mediated context and also their familiarity with those or similar images, rather than against any standard of suffering. For example, the paradox in tolerating images of the dead on our screens in crime shows and other reality programming and the revulsion to images of those killed 'in our name' appears greater now then ever.

Meanwhile, the images of atrocity that are part of our daily news diet – the 1990s televised blood of 'ethnic cleansing', the siege of Sarajevo and elsewhere in Bosnia, and the genocide in Rwanda, for example – appear to overwhelm many in the West as 'compassion fatigue' sets in (and this is not to mention the many conflicts around the globe that rarely pass a threshold of contemporary news values). But it is precisely a mediated separation between 'our' 'just' wars, and those of the 'other' and at a distance, which serves to legitimize warfare as an acceptable means of settling scores. The televising of the Gulf War and particularly the embedded correspondents covering the Iraq War helped establish a view from the eyeline of the aggressor as the dominant Western frame. As Peter Preston (2003) asks, 'What relevant guideline means we must watch guns blazing into a void of tactfully averted eyes?'

The televising of the Iraq War, probably more than any other conflict in history, fundamentally disconnected the machinery of warfare from the bloody consequences of its use. But even if the bodies were to be 'brought back in' to the visioning machine that is television, the result remains the same. Many of the documentaries, dramatizations and endless anniversary programming that followed soon after the Gulf War did not substantially reconfigure the existing television record. In media times the war was won, and the accumulation of footage from the invaders' point of view served to crystallize memory around this dominant TV experience.

The maximum exposure of the round-the-clock coverage of the Iraq War in the USA and UK conversely delivered the most sanitized pictures. Furthermore, the inevitable aftermath of saturation media coverage is simply less coverage. If the originally unseen or unbroadcast consequences of war are to emerge then they can only be afforded disproportionately less airtime after the event, and only in the drip, drip of news items and documentaries (and hardly in primetime schedules). After the 'end of hostilities' had been declared to the Iraq War, there was a rush of documentaries broadcast in the UK as if to acknowledge a shrinking window of relevance. After all, the 'media war' is most convincingly won or lost when most of the media are there and when most of the audience is watching.

An important question that changing modes and speeds of historicization raises is whether images in this environment still affect and move audiences in the same way. Or, does the repetition and re-representation over time of once-shocking images of the consequences of warfare serve to numb and anaesthetize? One of the principal justifications espoused for the display and publication of 'disturbing' images is that they act precisely to prevent amnesia and stand as a 'lesson of history' to demonstrate the futility and the horrors of warfare for future generations beyond living memory. Yet, does the repetition of key images (at the exclusion of others) iconize suffering and death so that they lose the impact they once had and thus the very purpose of their original capturing, publication and repeated mediation? Does familiarity with a picture, no matter how shocking, prevent further useful reflection on the event because it can too easily be read off the surface of the image, i.e. does it close down the possibility for future potentially more productive and/or alternative interpretations? Sontag (2003: 89) argues that this does not necessarily follow: 'Harrowing photographs do not inevitably lose their power to shock. But they are not much help if the task is to understand. Narratives can make us understand. Photographs do something else: they haunt us.'

And it is precisely these flashframes of memory (as I argue in the following chapter) that appear in television news as 'media templates', i.e. as ways of presenting current events with visual reference to those past events which news and programme editors deem to be similar. The media often skews present events in a narrative locked in a past that may constrain interpretations (and memory) rather than enable fresh understanding. The past, however, is not always presented as coherent, but often reassembled and juxtaposed as memorable image fragments.

Graphic photographs and images of warfare thus inhabit multiple news stories, times and contexts whose sum is far from an ordered and consistent narrative. So, harrowing photographs and footage may endure in memory, but the circumstances of those images and the story they once told may become detached through their repetition and familiarity. In this respect, as noted above, I identify a collapse of memory as our understanding of the past is overwhelmed by its mediated representations. According to Sontag, then,

> The problem is not that people remember through photographs, but that they remember only through the photographs. This remembering through photographs eclipses other forms of understanding and

remembering. To remember is, more and more, not to recall a story but to be able to call up a picture. (*ibid.*)

And it follows that iconic images, graphic or otherwise, have an even greater effect in eclipsing other forms of remembering. In this way, familiarity with an image or set of images, although sustaining a surface memory, can actually *limit* an understanding and engagement with the past.

In what follows I consider these issues as essentially concerning *conflicts* of memory over the Gulf Wars of 1991 and 2003. I explore how, increasingly, the actions of war enter publics' consciousness via the media at their inception, changing forever the nature of social and global understanding of events from distant battlefields. In doing so the media possess greater capacity – and seemingly greater authority – to shape memory, and, paradoxically, to simultaneously engineer its collapse. More than any other conflict before them, the Gulf Wars are subject to a mediation that affords them a tangible presence that is not peripheral to their history, but defining of it.

Chapter 2

From Vietnam to the Gulf – re-visions of war

MEMORY BEYOND THE LIVING ROOM

The Vietnam War – the 'first TV War' or 'living-room war' – was so named against assumptions about who was watching and how. It occurred during what was fast becoming the McLuhanesque era as the television set became dominant in the familial landscape of the home in the developed Western world. For as McLuhan himself argued, 'The public is now participant in every phase of the war, and the main actions of the war are now being fought in the American home itself' (McLuhan and Fiore, 2001/1968: 134). The living room was the space in which household members would cluster around the television and *be* an audience in the highly routinized times of news programmes. Television helped reproduce an illusion of mass – in advertising and marketing, in ways-to-bring-up-your-children, and in theories about the media. Ideas about the nature and unity of *the* audience inhabiting the American home drove perceptions of the impact and persuasiveness of the message delivered through television.

In this environment a television war could not fail to fulfil the early promise of the medium in sweeping middle America in its image(s), notably through graphic and daily pictures of the real and bloody consequences of war – including and especially in defeat – the memory of which would effect a caution in US military engagements, and in their relationship with television journalists, for years to come. And it is this interrelationship, and what later became an *intersection* between the military and the media, which is one of the concerns here.

This chapter sets out how a *new memory* of the Vietnam War has permeated military–media relations ever since, being re-visioned by and reflexively shaping the 1991 Gulf War, which, in turn, enabled a sequel of its own in the 2003 Iraq War. These late modern conflicts are subject to mass coverage by an increasingly visually-obsessed media which both shape *and* compete with human memory. In fact, human memory treats the past and present in a similar way to the news media. Todd Gitlin (1980: 49–50), for example, argues,

> Media are mobile spotlights, not passive mirrors of the society; selectivity is the instrument of their action. A news story adopts a certain frame and rejects or downplays material that is discrepant. A story is a choice, a way of seeing an event that also amounts to a way of screening from sight.

The human mind also 'works on' memory, transforming the past by keeping alive certain images and versions of events and suppressing or altering others. However, can the mediated image, fixed in the photograph or video, ever be subject to the same dynamics? How can the 'artificial' – the mediated memory of Vietnam, for instance – be transformed into an acceptable though tangible form by the American media?

New events enable the past to be represented in comparison with the present, as well as providing a frame – a particular way of viewing the present. Media templates perform this very function by selectively re-articulating the past at the same time as imposing an often image-based frame or narrative on the present. The Gulf War was the first opportunity that both the American military and media had to actively employ Vietnam as a template and in this way re-visualize it. Despite its extensive re-writing in print and in television documentary, the received history of the Vietnam War prior to 1991 appeared largely unaffected by media templates. Both the military and the media had yet to provide something of sufficient scale to obscure the haunting memory of Vietnam.

Living memory, to borrow a phrase from Paul Gilroy, involves negotiating 'the living memory of the changing same' (1993: 198). That is, the telling and retelling of stories 'serve[s] a mnemonic function: directing the consciousness of the group back to significant, nodal points in its common history and its social memory' (ibid.). Although Gilroy refers here to a particular articulation of memory – tradition[5] – this idea is useful in conceptualizing the mnemonic function of television. In US history the nodal point of the Vietnam War as mediated via television has in effect been retold in print and in movies ever since, and in terms of television news narratives most recently in the 1991 Gulf War. The living memory of the Vietnam War, given its longer historical trajectory than the Iraq Wars, has literally been remade in the artificial memory of the media more often. It is the latter, however, which more definitively entered into collective consciousness via television – as 'television events' that are more susceptible, both to remaking by the medium of their production, but also to those who possess living memory of them as viewers of the time. The negotiation of the social memory of warfare, therefore, is increasingly a matter concerning audiences.

However, as new memory is shaped by perceptions as much as by reality or history, it is important to underline that the perceived effects of the television coverage of the Vietnam War were based upon three flawed and related assumptions: firstly, the singularity of 'the' audience; secondly, its capacity to effect a change in military strategy and government policy; and thirdly, the actual proportion and unambiguous nature of graphic images of war shown on television at the time.

To expand this first point, generations of media theory and empirical research have yet to deliver a consistent or coherent assessment of the interpretations and behaviour of media audiences. By far the most sensible and perhaps radical account is by Abercrombie and Longhurst (1998), who imply that the audience is at best unknowable in their model of a 'diffused' audience. It seems better to begin with this admission and acknowledge the diversity of audiences – and to reference them more appropriately in the plural – than to try to identify uniform and collective responses to television events. For example, as Daniel C. Hallin (1986: 131) argues, 'Television images . . . pass very quickly, leaving the audience little time to reflect on their meaning . . . We know very little about how television audiences construct the meaning of what they see and hear.'

But in the years of the Vietnam War, television was only beginning to carve out a role for itself in American society, as were the politicians who attempted to harness its influence. In this respect the entanglement of television news with explanations of the outcome of the Vietnam War should be seen in the context of a medium in its infancy and a mythologizing of a mass audience. Yet, it is precisely the media and in particular television that have since ensured they remain 'written in' to a lasting narrative of Vietnam. The so-called first television war has actually become more significant in its televisual presence since *as* history than its effects or otherwise in the routinized and predictable news times in American homes of the 1960s and early 1970s. The medium may have been the message, but it is now, quite literally, history.

If coverage of the Vietnam War is remembered as conveying at least a tangible (if very limited) understanding of events, then the Gulf War signified a more abstract view of warfare, dominated by an obsession with on-screen visual effects, namely 'videographics'. In this respect 1991 witnessed the first TV video war. However, despite the TV coverage of Vietnam and the later Gulf Wars being inextricable from their respective and now entangled histories, what images actually dominate these accounts? If a new experience of warfare has been mediated by television, does this in a similar way forge a new memory of these conflicts, compared with earlier, less-mediated ones? In this chapter I contend that although television directs and refocuses memory, the enduring images of warfare are, paradoxically, *photographic* in nature. And, despite the transformations in televisuality – the whole view of warfare afforded by television – over the period from Vietnam to the present day, the visual flow and clutter of TV news more often obscures memory than it affords a defining image. Rather, definitive and enduring images are established through their remediation, repeated within ever-new news stories, yes on TV, but also in print and in other media as visual stills. And it is the fixed frames of the latter that come closer to resembling and being retained in human memory than the moving images within television and film footage.

THE JOURNALISTIC CONTEXT OF VIETNAM

Vietnam is often used as the benchmark of the widespread use of *actuality* footage in the televising of war, and the nature, extent and impact of this coverage inhabits a mythical presence in social memory. Rather than providing an informed understanding of events in Vietnam, particularly in the first few years of US military involvement, television routinely produced a highly contrived view. This often occurred due to a focus on the minutiae of war – on events that could be assembled and packaged to fit the structures of the evening news bulletins. Michael J. Arlen writing in *The New Yorker* in the late 1960s provides a critical account of journalistic practices of the time:

> Daily journalism in general seems to be virtually rooted in its tradi-tional single-minded way of presenting the actuality of daily life . . . It is now especially evident, and damaging, in Vietnam, where, for the most part, American journalism has practically surrendered itself to a consecutive, activist, piecemeal, the-next-day-the-First-Army-forged-onward-toward-Aachen approach to a war that even the journalists covering it know to be non-consecutive, non-activist, a war of silences . . . The journalists reorder the actuality of Vietnam into these isolated hard-news incidents for the benefit of their editors. (*1969: 114, 115*)

The short-lived but detailed images selected and packaged for the evening news give the illusion of evidence of war and particularly of mil-itary 'advances'. The reporting of each mini-event – a raid or a destruc-tion of an ammunitions dump, for example – signifies military progress: these are, after all, 'successful' acts captured on film. Crucially missing, however, is a significant and sustained contextualizing of these incidents and a sense of what the sum of all the actuality footage amounts to. The endless detail (as opposed to 'information') of actuality footage of bombing raid after bombing raid effected a coverage that became increasingly out-of-sync with the reality of the wider conflict. Thus, Arlen argues,

> most journalists here convey a more firmly realized picture of Vietnam in a couple of hours of conversation in the evening (with all those elisions made, the separate parts connected) than they've achieved (in complicity with their editors and their public) in six months of filing detached, hard-news reports. (*1969: 110*)

The 'reordering' of the images of war produced a version that fitted the predominant televisual network form of evening news of 22-and-a-half-minutes.[6] The news-cycles of this era were geared around recorded reports edited and simplified to fit a couple of minutes of air time (see Gitlin, 1980). In this way it was the conventions and structures of news reporting in addition to a lack of wider understanding of events by journalists that contributed to a very limited televisual perspective on the war.

However, even with (and perhaps because of) the packaging of 'successful' events and positive briefings in highly structured news programmes, the façade of a war 'going well' was not sustainable. Eventually, in the last few years of the war, as Donald L. Shaw and Shannon E. Martin point out, 'editors began to listen to their own reporters more than they did to the things-are-going-great messages they heard from the White House and Pentagon' (1993: 56). In this way it was the American communication system which could not maintain 'unnaturally monistic' relations between the media, government and the public for very long (p. 57). The discrepancies between the distant reality of events in Vietnam and the home rhetoric of official sources were brought into focus over time by a pluralistic media. It is unsurprising, therefore, that those of junior military rank in Vietnam who by 1991 had acquired considerable influence in media–military relations would ensure that press access to operations in the Gulf War would be tightly managed.

PHOTOGRAPHIC MEMORY – VIETNAM

The Vietnam War represents a disjuncture in memory. The mythologizing of television's responsibility for 'losing' the Vietnam War by politicians, pundits and presidents has been well and truly exposed in numerous publications since (e.g. notably Gitlin, 1980, Braestrup, 1983/1977 and Hallin, 1986). Yet this rewriting of the nature and impact of the TV coverage has not effected a change in the social memory of the relationship between television news images and the humiliation of the American military and government in Vietnam. For example, only a small percentage of film reports shown on television news during the conflict depicted actual fighting and graphic scenes of the dead or wounded (see, for example, Braestrup, 1983/1977 and Hallin, 1986). Yet, it is these visual images that haunt the mediated memory of Vietnam today.

The repetitive and drama-driven news environments of modern media perpetuate often narrow and simplistic versions of events. Images of the dramatic and the extraordinary (as well as those that are reminiscent of other previous 'stock'[7] images) become iconic at the expense of the mundane and the representative. The indelible visual images of Vietnam that have been disproportionately recycled in documentaries, in art and in museums endure precisely because they were once viewed as exceptional – simply as being more memorable. For most readers merely the title of some of the defining photos from Vietnam will be enough to trigger the image – 'Vietnam Napalm' by Nick Ut (1972) or 'The Execution' by Eddie Adams (1968). And for all the claims made about Vietnam as the first television war, it is the *photographic* images that endure. What can be considered as 'flashframes'[8] of memory – the freezing in time and space of a never-to-be-repeated moment and its capture in a single image – seem to carry greater cultural and historical weight than the moving image. In the words of Adams[9] on his photograph of the execution of a Vietcong by a South Vietnamese soldier, 'The bullet hit his head as the picture was taken'; a split-second earlier or later and this image would not have entered the mediated memory of the Vietnam War. Furthermore, the execution was also filmed by a camera crew and part of this footage appeared on the evening news; however, as Susan D. Moeller (1999) argues,

> the still images lingered in the memories because people could look at them as long as they wanted – they could go back to them and people really had an opportunity to linger on them in a way they couldn't linger on television. And so they were seared into people's brains in the way that television just couldn't be.[10]

In some ways, this statement reveals some of the contradictions inherent in what I have called 'new memory'. Our everyday understanding of human memory is something that is stored in our brain – 'seared' in Moeller's terms – as if permanently inscribed at some moment in time so that we may always 'see' the image. However, in reality, images only 'linger' in the memory as long as they are gone back to and re-introduced from their external and mediated existence; memories are always having to be re-made in the present. For example, Ulric Neisser (1982: 45) writes that,

> memories become flashbulbs primarily through the significance that is attached to them *afterwards*: later that day, the next day, and in subsequent months and years. What requires explanation, after all, is not the immediate survival of the memory . . . but its long endurance.

And it is the medium of the photograph that effects a permanence – a purposeful capturing of a single moment that even stills taken from moving film cannot compete with. A photograph – or its copy – on display in albums, galleries or exhibitions inhabits a very different physical space to the moving image. Its physicality affords the photograph a historical status that the television image has for many years been deprived of. The medium of film, however, does have a greater historical presence than television, partly because the traditional mechanics of its production are greater and seemingly more deliberate than those of television. It is a perception of television's greater ephemerality (as well as its trivializing nature) than either photography or film that contributes to a continued disguising of its *documenting* function. Television is rarely afforded the status of historical document.

The irony of Vietnam as the first television war is that a historical consciousness of the conflict is weighted in its photographic images. Although these still images do endure partly because of their later remediation through other media and particularly via television, they are nonetheless photographs – and are recognized as such by audiences. Although the residue of the memory of an event clings to the means of production of its images to some extent, it is the still images that pervade the media and social memory.

However, it can be said that those most iconic photographic images of this era tend to possess a cinematic quality. Nick Ut's 'Vietnam Napalm', for example, looks like a scene straight out of a Hollywood movie with children and soldiers fleeing on a road from hell. Its cinematic feel is accentuated through its deep spatial perspective – of a road disappearing into a burning horizon of dense smoke. The photograph captures a genuine snapshot of the horror of warfare on the faces of the children running towards the camera. Its endurance today as an iconic image of Vietnam reveals a great deal about the nature of memory in our highly videographic age, and particularly when compared with images that have not remained in the collective consciousness in the same way.

Obviously, as a black-and-white image, it automatically possesses a certain gravitas of depth and time. Paul Grainge (2002: 76), for example, argues, 'A quality of authenticity is ascribed to monochrome. It is part of a tradition of photojournalism that is able – and supposedly denied by the rapid flow and headline repetitions of CNN – to "probe the inner life of things".' Repetition, or rather, remediation, as I have suggested, is an essential dynamic of new memory. Nick Ut's photograph is recognizable to audiences today (some of whom were not born when it was taken) because of its remediation on television, in print and on the internet. The official recognition Ut received by way of winning the 1972 Pulitzer Prize ensured that 'Vietnam Napalm' entered a certain institutional memory. But it also endures by way of the autobiographical (and living) memory of Kim Phuc, the girl in the photograph, whose life-story post-Vietnam has acquired a historical interest of its own and has been the subject of media documentaries and news features.

The numerous strands of the remediation of Nick Ut's photograph uniquely contribute to its historical trajectory and to its retention in social memory. It is difficult to isolate all the factors which contribute to one photograph's iconic status and not to other, potentially equally powerful, images. Inevitably, there is a self-fulfilling prophecy to the process of iconization. This has even led to some museum curators seeking and displaying the unfamiliar to at least provide balance to the potentially visual straightjacking of reinforcing a very limited popular history of already familiar images.[11]

PHOTOGRAPHIC MEMORY – GULF WAR

Sontag describes her own visual memory in an interview with the *Boston Review* in June 1975:

> what I remember of a movie amounts to an anthology of single shots. I can recall the story, lines of dialogue, the rhythm. But what I remember visually are selected moments that I have, in effect, reduced to stills. It's the same for one's own life. Each memory from one's childhood, or from any period that's hot in the immediate past, is like a still photograph rather than a strip of film.[12]

It is 'selected moments' that, despite all the relentless movement and 'flow' of television, are still elicited from the medium. To return to a photographic metaphor, televisual memory is reduced to flashframes over time. Despite the videographic excess and indulgent graphics that characterized TV's presentation of the Gulf War, some of the most enduring and iconic images are photographic, if not cinematic, in nature, rather than inherently televisual. The burning Kuwaiti oil wells and the oil-drenched sea bird, for example, as much as the videographics, function to symbolically represent the war, the fighting, and the dead. These are some of the acceptable icons of the global memory of this war in our mediated age. The green nightscape pyrotechnics which look like an extension of TV's videographic environment have also endured. However, one problem with TV's own repetition of the Gulf War is that the videographics and the CNN environment of 1991 today appear somewhat dated. Instead, it is the photographic images, as with the medium of cinema, which tend to accrue more historical gravitas with time. A perception of a 'trivializing' medium, after all, will always restrict television's role in providing no more than 'trivial' history. Its images that can be viewed as and through other media, however, are more likely to emerge in social memory as stills – as photographs in the mind.

Some of the few images extensively mediated in the West that depicted the brutality of warfare included seven Coalition POWs captured by Iraq and paraded on Iraqi television. Most significant for American audiences was a US pilot whose face was marked through ejection from his plane and/or torture by his Iraqi captors. Stills taken from the TV footage of visibly bruised and apparently disillusioned pilots appeared across the fronts of national newspapers and magazines around the globe. The transference from one medium to another degraded the grainy images further and accentuated the POW's visible scars. In respect of the American pilot, Douglas Kahn (1992: 45) observes, 'the transfer from video to photolith left his face further lacerated and numbed by raster lines'. The remediation of these images in print in this way afforded them a more significant (photographic) status.

The *Guardian* of 21 January 1991, for example, reproduced these images across the top of its front page, and although clearly being sourced from television, they revealed little evidence of the highly videographic environment in which the Gulf War was framed.[13] Their poor reproduction gave them a more sinister look, as though taken from an old Hollywood black-and-white B-movie.

The flickering video of the Coalition POWs shown on Iraqi TV on 20 January 1991, and rebroadcast on CBS and CNN and networks around the world, looked like film from a different age, with little colour and shot against a whitish background. The resonance of the 1991 POW images in social memory, however, as with their presentation in the *Guardian*, is as black-and-white stills. Twelve years later, images of American POWs shown on Iraqi TV on 23 March 2003, and rebroadcast on Al-Jazeera and around the world (but not by most US networks), appeared across nearly all the UK newspaper front pages the following day.[14] All of these were stills taken from Al-Jazeera TV and reproduced in colour, with some newspapers leaving the channel's icons and other framing visible (as in the *Mirror* example in Figure 3 below) but most cropping the separate images so the face of each POW filled the frame. The images that carry with them more signs of the medium of their production, i.e. as 'screen grabs', afford a different effect as they more closely resemble the televisual than the photographic. The nature of remediation importantly influences the impact of images and their existence in social memory. Sontag (2003: 105–6) for example, argues that,

> an image is drained of its force by the way it is used, where and how often it is seen. Images shown on television are by definition images of which, sooner or later, one tires. What looks like callousness has its origin in the instability of attention that television is organized to arouse and to satiate by its surfeit of images . . . A more reflective engagement with content would require a certain intensity of awareness – just what is weakened by the expectations brought to images disseminated by the media, whose leaching out of content contributes most to the deadening of feeling.

The drive to capture a definitive and iconic image is much more difficult under circumstances of intensive competition and extensive mediation. The cyclical nature of the mass mediation of images tends to render many potentially defining images unexceptional. However, an image may actually be selected for broadcast or publication because of its similarity to another, already-recognizable image, or stand out because it 'connects' with a familiar image in one's own memory (see p. 135).

VIDEOGRAPHIC AMNESIA – GULF WAR

The Gulf War produced a near inversion of Vietnam television coverage in that proportionately greater time allocated in the relative duration of the former simply did not afford more images of war. Or, at least it can be said that it did not provide actuality images that were familiar to US audiences whose prior nodal reference point of war on television was Vietnam. Instead, military and political news briefings did afford some structure and daily regularity to events shown on television. But, with the exception of the extraordinary audio-only coverage from Baghdad, mostly contrived pool footage and talking heads dominated the CNN vision of this war. Late into the night, CNN often broadcast random satellite footage as it came in, i.e. without editing or providing explanatory audio commentary. However, as with the comparatively routinized coverage of Vietnam, the relentlessness of a parade of images and talking heads did not afford a coherent or critical view of the war.

Instead, a highly *stylized* view of war was managed, both by the Pentagon and the news networks. As Caldwell (1995: 289) argues, 'As viewers watched amorphous, electronically smeared, and monochromatic imagery, Pentagon briefers carried on overly detailed and comprehensive descriptions of what the audience was *supposed* to see.' As with Vietnam there occurred a disjuncture between the apparent detail carried by (in this case) continuous coverage, and a genuine comprehension of the progress of the war. Yet, unlike Vietnam, the Gulf War was over before much actuality (non-pool) footage could contaminate the stylistic endeavours of network television. Hugh Herbert (1991), a *Guardian* journalist, for example, acknowledges the fundamental limits of the televising of the war:

> All the obvious highlights of live TV had the self-destructive element of stage-management. All soon were seen to have misled us. Deception was endemic to the Gulf . . . Coverage of these outwardly dramatic events was swamped by interpretation, attempts to make sense out of a ransacked filing system.

This post-war analysis made clear that nose-cone video carried by missiles and 'precision' bombing would not, in itself, again be permitted to win a television war. By the end of the decade, in the war over Kosovo, NATO military briefers and spokesmen were faced with an audience and a press much less inclined to consume the video pyrotechnics at face value.

As stated above, the Gulf War was dominated by a videographic style of news presentation on television. This is merely part of what Caldwell defines as 'televisuality' – 'a stylizing performance – an exhibitionism that utilized many different looks' (1995: 5):

> programs intentionally engage the viewer with *multiple* and *simultaneous* layers of perceptual and discursive information, many times overwhelming him or her by combining visual, spatial, gestural, and iconic signals. Televisuality is, in this sense, a phenomenon of communicative and *semiotic over-abundance*. (*1995: 362n35, original emphasis*)

The superimposition of logos, icons and various other images and texts, all contribute to television news' environment. Videographic style goes much deeper though than mere on-screen graphics, with a consciousness of the 'televisual apparatus' itself. This includes banks of monitors and screens-within-the-screen and the production of simultaneity through multiple satellite feeds distributed to different visual frames that split the screen into desktop-sized fragments of different times and places. The co-ordination of these with the televised image of the news anchor, and other talking heads, has been defined as the 'CNN look' (Bolter and Grusin, 1999: 189; see also Hoskins, 2001a).

Videographic presentation involves the televisual re-consumption of its own coverage – a 'celebration' by network news of what it has already delivered. CNN's 1991 success, even to the extent that it has become synonymous with the war, is something that was not lost to the network. In fact CNN clung to their own memory of their coverage almost obsessively throughout the 1990s and particularly when Saddam pushed himself back onto the news agenda in various cat-and-mouse games with the UNSCOM weapons' inspectors. Their re-consumption of the opening of the war onto the global media stage was immediately commodified in the form of a promotional trailer. CNN repackaged various audio fragments mostly taken from the al-Rashid Hotel reporting and put them to a completely black screen. The trailer employed white text appearing in the centre of the screen rather than using spoken narration. Table 1 sets out the trailer and shows how a mix of times and places has been assembled to provide a taster of CNN's reporting of the early days of the war.

Even at this early stage CNN has identified the Baghdad reports as a significant part of their success and in this example montages these

Table 1: Visual and audio text and original location of live broadcast and recording from CNN *World News* Gulf War promotional trailer, broadcast 19 January 1991

Visual text (White words on a black screen)	Audio	Original location of recording
	Bernard Shaw (Reporter): *Something is happening . . .*	al-Rashid Hotel, Baghdad
The eyes	*. . . outside.* **(Unknown):** *flash! . . . confirm! . . . explosion!*	al-Rashid Hotel, Baghdad
The ears	**Charles Jaco** (Reporter): *There are sounds of planes overhead, we don't know whose planes they are, but . . .*	Unidentified air-base, Dhahran, Saudi Arabia
Of the world	*. . . air raid sirens!* **Colleen Jackson** (Wife of US Navy Serviceman): *I'm scared.*	Dhahran, as above. Outside a church, Norfolk Virginia
	Tom Mintier (Reporter): *They're all waiting, for some type of word.*	
CNN The World's News Leader	**Shaw**: *It has been a long night for us . . . a night some of us will never forget.*	Baghdad, as above

elements with reporting of reactions from relatives of those serving in the US forces in the Gulf. The use of the black screen effectively 'closes down' the visual, providing an aura of night, with audio fragments emphasizing both the drama and uncertainty of events up until that point in the war. In this way the trailer strips away much of the intensely visual elements of the videographic domain, especially in respect of colour, excessive icons and moving images, but nonetheless recombines temporally and spatially distantiated fragments.[15] The monochromatic contrast is highly effective, appearing in the midst of CNN's videographic enveloping of the war and is also a means of representing its audio-only coverage from Baghdad.

The studio environment of the time provided much more opportunity for graphics and visual effects, particularly in *representations* of events and places. This can be said to have complemented Pentagon-produced imagery, but with the same effect – standing in for the mostly absent actuality footage of the war. Television news studios themselves became virtual representations of the spaces of the war (and particularly the battlefield), massively simplifying issues, action and the consequences of warfare. ABC News, for example, constructed a studio-sized landscape for the presenter Peter Jennings to literally walk over. The programme *A Line in the Sand*, broadcast on 10 September 1990, considered the likely scenarios ahead during the build-up of what was then labelled the 'Gulf Crisis'. The *A Line in the Sand* visual still of the sunset/rise over an expanse of desert evoked the deadline set by President Bush for Saddam to withdraw his armies from their occupation of Kuwait. This programme was broadcast at an early phase in the conflict, when the US audience was still learning about the region and being prepared for the prospect of war. The protracted build-up to war on television was used to sell the idea of the necessity for military action using partly real and partly virtual spaces. The images of sunset and sunrise over the desert used in this programme were typical of US coverage and were interspersed with virtual representations. The sense of the passage of time is conveyed in the progamme itself with 'night' falling over the 'Middle East'. Jennings, silhouetted, actually walks off the darkened set to leave an empty place (i.e. empty desert) full of anticipation of the war to come at the end of the programme.

The relationship constructed between the here-and-now (the shared studio space with presenter and audience) and the there-and-now (the desert of the Middle East) is intrinsically part of the view constructed through televisual apparatuses of the time. The shrinking of the Middle East in this form of representation provides a highly simplistic mapping of the region, as does Jennings' (1990) accompanying discourse:

So all over the Middle East tonight just like all over America people are wondering what is going to happen in the Middle East next. If you heard the President speaking to a joint session of Congress earlier this evening you heard him say again he's not going to let this aggression against Kuwait stand . . . There are options. We've got just a couple of minutes left and we'll probably leave out something. But let's consider some of them.

This symbolic representation is a feature of the videographic news environment that provides an abstract perception of people, places and events. The intersection between the military and the media over time has assisted in providing a 'derealized' perception of war, that is further and further away from the site of its action. Michael J. Shapiro, for example, draws upon the work of Virilio (1989) and defines 'derealization' as, 'the process by which increasingly abstract and distancing modes of symbolic representation mediate the relationships through which persons and places acquire meanings' (1997: 88).

In later years, television news reoriented its visual scale with the widespread use of often larger-than-life screens within the studio and even, as with Sky News, an entire 'videowall'. Presenters in 2003 (as with Jennings, above) could literally stride around and in front of images that overwhelmed their physical presence.

One of the consequences of the seeming *unreality* of the televising of the war, as with any 'television event', is that it does not inhabit much of a historical space outside of its televisual mediation. The historical event appears to carry with it the trappings of the essentially ephemeral and fleeting TV image. Cumings (1992: 103), for example, argues, 'Remember the Gulf War? Or was that last season's hit show? The Gulf War was a war fought to demolish a memory, but it was also a war that produced no memory.' Videographics helped to convey an unreal (and highly sanitized) war and in this way the more tangible connections to warfare reside in those images that, as I have suggested, are captured (and re-mediated since) in the photographic. Televisuality literally 'screened out' the Gulf War and, as with Vietnam, the received TV experience has a sometimes contradictory relationship with social memory and with history itself.

LIVING MEMORIES VERSUS MEDIA MEMORIES

For example, one need only examine a seemingly modern media obsession with those who are the 'last surviving' men or women, who witnessed or took part in a particular event, the significance of which is shown through some kind of public commemoration. For example, in the future, one can envisage the 'last survivors' of the attacks on the US on September 11, 2001, being prompted for their recollection of these events on the anniversaries of these tragedies. Quite simply, the smaller their number, the more valuable their contribution to living memory becomes; the implication being that some kind of diminishment of the memory of the historical event will occur with the passing away of the keepers of human memory. The importance associated with this kind of co-presence at an event, and later collective recollection of the event, is similar to Durkheim's notion of the diminishing of the 'social force' in relation to the ending of co-presence of the group. Yet, it is the circumstances of new memory which increasingly provide a memory so vivid and visual in the present, and in ever new present moments, that living memory appears increasingly to be usurped and commodified in and through the ubiquitous electronic media archive.

Only six months after the tragedy of September 11, 2001, for example, this event was already described as 'the most documented event in history'.[16] Perhaps equally, the Iraq War was mediated via television and the internet to such an extent that the living memory of the many civilians, military and newsworkers who bore witness to this conflict will not only be competing with the endless documentation captured by the media, but the media will be its principal means of articulation and dissemination. The original (i.e. real-time) and excessive mediation (and remediation) of these events poses one of the challenges of new memory. That is to say that the media leaves little space in or through which alternative and potentially contradictory framings of the past can enter into collective consciousness.

Put another way, how can human memory thrive and compete with the vast capacity of the media archive, unaided or unhindered by the relative stasis of the visually-driven mass media? Rose outlines this problem in respect of what he terms 'artificial' memories:

> They have become part of our 'shared history'. But, equally, we can no longer make and remake them in our own minds, assimilate them fully into our lived experience and consciousness, because they are for ever fixed by the video. Further, the power of the camera and the film-maker allows history – that is, collective memory – to be remade . . . The new technologies offer unrivalled prospects for, on the one hand, artificial memory, and on the other, the production of completely fabricated memories . . . (*1993: 98*)

In this way, the balance of society's 'retention of its past' can be seen shifting further away from the fundamentally flawed although dynamic and living human memory, to one that is reduced to iconic images. For example, one of the enduring memories for audiences of the opening of the Gulf War, live on CNN, is the green 'nightscape' footage of Baghdad with Iraqi tracer-fire shooting upward as Coalition bombs hitting targets around the city show up as bright flashes. Here is an extract of an account from an unidentified US male viewer of his memory of the beginning of the bombardment against Iraq on television: 'I'll never forget. I was watching television, and all of a sudden: "We interrupt . . ." and so forth, and over Baghdad, and then came these green shots and the war had started. And oh, from that point on it was almost a constant thing.'[17] This remembering is interesting by way of its inaccuracy. The viewer describes film footage of Baghdad which was not available to any Western television network for broadcast until a couple of days after the war had started. Indeed, one of the ironies of CNN's coverage of the Gulf War (which was fed to other networks around the globe) was that its most intensive instantaneous transmissions occurred in the opening of the war on 16 January 1991, and were fed live in audio only (see Philip M. Taylor, 1998/1992: 8 and Hoskins, 2001a: 219–20). Within a couple of days, Peter Arnett's CNN voice was dubbed onto ITV's and ABC's eerie footage which was filmed – but not transmitted – at the very opening of Operation Desert Storm. Effectively, the news narrative had been reconstituted for the visual medium and it is this 'version' that has been repeatedly replayed since, replacing the less visually appealing images of maps of Baghdad that accompanied the original CNN real-time audio, as illustrated in Figure 1.

It is the green nightscape footage over Baghdad[18] that has come to define the televisual record, and the new memory of the first Gulf War. Other images have become equally iconic: burning oil wells; the flash of US Patriot missiles being fired from ships in the Gulf; and, of course, Saddam Hussein himself (the televisual construction of whom is the subject of Chapter 5). But all of these have become fixed in the minds of viewers through their repetition since, on television, film, the internet and in print. The actual experience of audiences watching the opening couple of days of the war live on CNN was predominantly of reporters and other 'talking heads' on rooftops, outside 'airbases', at military and Pentagon briefings, and, of course, in the studio. What was remarkable about CNN's reporting at the time was that it was, somewhat fortuitously, the only network with reporters in Baghdad able to report the

Figure 1   Real-time coverage
Peter Arnett, Bernard Shaw and John Holliman transmitted live in audio-only
from the al-Rashid Hotel, Baghdad, CNN, 16 January 1991

opening of a war live, using a satellite phone, along with Peter Arnett were Bernard Shaw and John Holliman, all reporting from a ninth-floor room of the al-Rashid Hotel, central Baghdad. Much of their talk 'down the line' to CNN Centre in Atlanta and around the globe involved detailed description of 'what they could see', that is the broadcast talk more commonly to be found on radio.

Their own field of vision, however, was restricted to dark hotel rooms and a literally blacked-out skyline of the city. Virtually the only illumination available to them was the tracer-fire of Iraqi anti-aircraft guns and the explosions caused by the bombs dropped by Coalition bombers. It is a description of precisely this view that occupied a large amount of their extended commentary. For example:

Peter Arnett: There's all this anti-aircraft fire in our vicinity, but the explosions, this one a huge red-rose explosion, probably ten miles away lighting up the sky.

John Holliman: I'm going back to the window 'cause I see some bright lights off to just one direction from our location and I see more and more air burst and it looks like a hundred fire flies off in the south-west of where we are now . . . The fire flies are flashing brightly one after another, it's like sparklers on the fourth of July at a great, great distance many miles from where we are. The blast that came through this window a few minutes ago was very much like the first blast you feel when you're out at the countdown clock at Cape Canaveral for a space shuttle launch. It was just a powerful wave of hot air that came into our location here – and the sky is still alight . . . I'm going to look out of the window and see where this bright light is coming from. (*CNN, live, 16 January 1991*)

The relatively restricted space of the al-Rashid hotel rooms and the view afforded to the CNN journalists became the focus of the opening two days of the war for this network and for the channels around the globe taking CNN feeds. Furthermore, the apparent immediacy and instantaneity of the experience (which I examine in Chapter 3) aided support for the war in this early stage as it appeared to offer a unique experience in the reporting of conflict. Even Arnett, a seasoned war correspondent, drew attention to the cinematic effect: 'It has to be unique in journalistic history to have a front-row seat at one of the great air bombardments of history' (CNN, live, 16 January 1991). Although compelling for audiences the audio-only initial reporting heralded a characteristic of the war that has obsessed scholars ever since, notably the *unreal* nature of the television experience. Television (even when like radio) provided a safe proximity to conflict, quite simply a view of at least something, somewhere, that was happening *now*. And to many audiences the newness of 24-hour television news offered a *continuous* news event that appeared unbounded by the routines and structures of television schedules and their daily lives.

The problem with allocating round-the-clock coverage to a news event, however, was that in 1991, the information-flow about the war rarely kept pace with the televisual news-flow. Consequently, much of the television coverage consisted of the recycling of earlier images and endless speculation by talking heads about what *might* happen later that hour or day. Even the reporters in the al-Rashid Hotel in the heart of Baghdad were faced with long periods when simply nothing was happening and they thus had to endlessly repeat their accounts and to speculate about events ahead and elsewhere. Furthermore, the pool reporting system which restricted the numbers of journalists in the Gulf and what they could see and report on effectively homogenized film reports into very particular views or shots of military action. The combined effect of these phenomena produced what was decried at the time and since as a highly 'sanitized' view of warfare and its conse-quences. Baudrillard, for example, has provided some of the most vociferous commentary in this respect. He describes what he claims to be the

> professional and functional stupidity of those who pontificate in perpetual commentary on the event . . . the CNN types . . . who make us experience the emptiness of television as never before . . . no one will hold this expert or general or that intellectual for hire to account for the idiocies or absurdities proffered the day before, since these will be erased by those the following day. In this manner, everyone is amnestied by the ultra-rapid succession of phony events and phony discourses. (*1991: 51*)

Clearly, this perspective affords little hope for the prospects of a meaning-ful comprehension of the event by TV audiences, nor for the production of a lasting memory. Yet, despite the *amnesia* of audiences that Baudrillard and other theorists of the media claim is a by-product of the television experience of the Gulf War, the actual living memory of this conflict involves people's relationship with the medium itself. Part of the compulsion of the viewing experience of the reports from the al-Rashid Hotel was that global audiences became real-time witnesses themselves of this quite unique coverage of war. And, although the video may fix the image in artificial memory, individual memory may possess more freedom than Rose (above) suggests, by virtue of their temporal and spatial relationship to the mediated event.

MEDIA TEMPLATES – VIETNAM TO THE GULF

One of the key dynamics of human memory is the retelling of past experienced events. Of course, if we go far back enough in history to oral cultures, we find that face-to-face story-telling was the principal vehicle of the passage of history between peoples and in the forging of social memory. In our mediated age, however, storytelling contributes much more than just a linear historical narrative, for it reflexively impinges upon and alters events in the present.

Television, as the medium mistakingly charged with losing the Vietnam War, and some of the same journalists and former military men later described as TV 'experts', had most to gain from the successful prosecution and presentation of the Gulf War. Although many journalists would be happy to be attributed the influence conferred by their presence in Vietnam, regardless of the actual outcome of war, events in the Gulf presented the first major opportunity since the early 1970s for the media to reshape perceptions of their role in covering warfare. What it is important to point out is the absolute interpenetration of the Vietnam War with the Gulf War in the minds and practices of the US government, military and media. This was no more evident than in the rhetoric of the then Commander-in-Chief speaking live to a global audience at and on the outbreak of war:

> I've told the American people before that this will not be another Vietnam and I repeat this here tonight: our troops will have the best possible support in the entire world and they will not be asked to fight with one hand tied behind their back. I'm hopeful that this fighting

will not go on for long and that casualties will be held to an absolute minimum. This is an historic moment. (*George Bush, 16 January 1991*)

In this way, one can draw direct comparison between an individual attempting to alter, suppress or forget altogether painful pieces of his or her past, with attempts to reconstruct history in the light of the present as a collective project. This is perhaps most evident in time of war, when a sense of collective identity and unity can be heightened in the form of patriotism. Despite the primary objective of 'liberating Kuwait' from Iraqi occupation, US public discourse was driven by a determination to reassert the country's position as a global military force in the present, and for the future, in comparison with the failures of the past. This required purging the record – the social memory – of the past in Vietnam, through successful military performance in the present and through proclaimed intended actions in the future. In the example above, President Bush invokes the past as a pretext for present actions but also as a form of historical revisionism in constructing the US military engagement in Vietnam as unfair.

This kind of historical working and contextualization from a US president is not surprising and one could say that this is a common form of political discourse, not least because politicians like to talk up the historical significance of their actions. The historical framing of events by the media, however, as I reference elsewhere in this account, although routine, is perhaps less visible. More significant is that journalists are increasingly writing themselves into the history of the events they report on. In recent times, and particularly during the Iraq War, reporters have become increasingly on-camera, in-the-frame, and inextricable from the story they claim to be telling (a phenomenon I explore in detail below). This is partly connected to developments in the *visual style* of television and that which Caldwell (above) refers to as 'televisuality'. However, the real dynamic driving the intertwining of reporter with reported is simply that in relation to the event they were *there*.

Throughout history, journalists have sought out eyewitness testimony of events reported as news. To have witnessed, or rather *experienced*, an event, conveys a certain status on the story-teller as primary source. Personal testimony conveys authority and credibility to the speaker whether they witnessed a street crime and are retelling their account in a court of law, or were present at the fall of the Berlin Wall and are contributing to one of the countless television documentaries on the historic events of 1989. To say 'I was there', however, affords a status beyond that of merely material witness. Individual human memory, as we have seen, is highly flawed and transforms over time (unlike the photograph or video-still). So the accuracy of these accounts based upon human memory is highly questionable – people routinely *mis*-remember – and so it is their co-presence or some other relation to the event that affords legitimacy to their account beyond that of human memory alone.

Throughout the US media coverage of the Gulf War the Vietnam War was frequently used as a *template* to frame events that were often unfolding in real-time. Frequent repetition and re-framing of key TV images extends the past into the present in new ways, creating templates with which to measure the present. Templates are also constructed through journalistic talk and their often routine contextualizing of the present with reference to a past event. Jenny Kitzinger, for example, argues, 'Whereas a frame is envisaged as a "map" or "window"' which can show different paths and perspectives, the template event implies a more rigid and precisely outlined perspective (which both *operates within*, and *contributes to*, a *specific* substantive frame' (2000: 75). Televisual templates thus contribute to providing relatively 'fixed' ways of reporting on and seeing news events and are particularly powerful when drawn from journalists' personal experiences.

For CNN and other Western television networks, having journalists who were actually in and around Vietnam at the time of the war provided an ideal source for comparison in their reporting from the Gulf, because they had been *there*. Peter Arnett, for example, one of CNN's three correspondents in Baghdad on the first night of the Coalition strikes (and who has since become synonymous with the televisual record of the conflict), was also a war correspondent, working for Associated Press, in Vietnam. Live from Baghdad, Arnett claims to recall his experience then, and compares it to the conflict unfolding around him:

> I couldn't help thinking as I heard the distant bombs punctuating President Bush's speech [of] his reference to . . . 'this will not be another Vietnam'. And I was thinking back to Vietnam where I spent many years, to a similar raid in 1972, a B52 strike on Hanoi, the inter-

esting thing was that raid came . . . near the end of the Vietnam War and many say it helped end that war. This raid on Baghdad and else-where in this region tonight is at the beginning of this war and maybe it certainly won't be a 'Vietnam'. (*CNN, live, 16 January 1991*)

An uncertainty amongst many commentators as to the likely nature of Operation Desert Storm at its launch is evident in Arnett's qualified dis-course, e.g. 'maybe it certainly won't be . . .'. Nonetheless, the Vietnam comparison evoked by Bush and by journalists signalled from the begin-ning that this was the historical yardstick by which the Gulf War was to be measured. President Bush's intention that this would 'not be another Vietnam' could also be construed as a determination that the Gulf would not *look* like another Vietnam. In direct contrast, coverage outside the USA did not necessarily have to share the sensibilities of the US networks, in terms of its visual matching of past and present stories. The French National network TF1, for example, on the same day as Arnett's spoken comparison, provided a series of visual comparisons drawn from the eight-year Iran–Iraq War and from Vietnam in their coverage of the capturing of Coalition pilots by Iraq. This included Iraqi TV pictures of Iranian POWs and INA television pictures of American POWs in Vietnam. In this way an instant visual narrative and historical context was produced, and today visual templates are used routinely by television news networks. These include image montages that impose simple historical narratives on a news story, often drawing upon stock images that have been recycled by television and other news media over a period of time.

Although individual journalistic narratives appear to offer the oppor-tunity of the dynamics and flaws that are characteristic of human memory, their accounts are nonetheless anchored by the visual images that drive television news. In this way even the authority conveyed by personal testimony is literally mediated by the availability of matching visual images which literally close down the possibilities for interpreta-tion. Much of the US television news talk of Vietnam during 1990 and 1991 can be considered in some ways as quite liberating because of its disconnection from the visual images that haunted American audiences over many years. This includes those who didn't witness the media images from Vietnam at the time but who have nonetheless lived in the historical shadow of the mythology of the first television war. In using an aural-only framing of Vietnam, a more sanitized and palatable discourse is circulated via the television news environment – almost as though this was revisionist therapy, only on our TV screens. Arnett (as above and at other times during CNN's coverage) places his recollections of Vietnam into the visually 'safe' frame of his audio-only transmissions from Baghdad. In this way television news templates can function reflexively to reshape or at least recontextualize their historical subject matter as well as to impose old contexts and frames on new events.

Vietnam, however, was used as a visual template on an ABC News Special in January 1991. A four-minute pre-recorded report compares the development of the peace protests during Vietnam with their apparently greater support and momentum in response to the outbreak of the Gulf War. In addition to the reporter's comparison and that provided by the contributions of various peace campaigners and commentators, the report opens with stock film footage of Vietnam. This is in colour and depicts some iconic imagery of US troops jumping from a helicopter hovering just above the ground and others firing machine-guns and mortars at an unseen enemy. It also includes a close-up of the face of presumably a US soldier evidently in some pain. The footage shot in Vietnam ends with a view of Americans ascending ladders up to a hovering transport helicopter and a shot of (the legs of) an injured soldier being half-dragged on a makeshift stretcher by his companions, away from the camera. The next scene is of a large group of chanting and arm waving protestors gathered in a square. These images are literally 'fast-forwarded' (as indicated in the transcript in Figure 2) to stock nightscape footage of Baghdad illuminated by explosions and tracer-fire.

Judd's report aired during ABC's continuing coverage employs a media template of Vietnam both in terms of the contributors' remarks and the direct visual comparison. The use of the Vietnam footage is also interesting, however, by way of its highly simplistic framing of the war. The stock images here construct a highly condensed and closed narrative version of America's involvement in Vietnam: troops are airlifted in, shoot at unseen enemy, suffer casualties, retreat and are airlifted out. This template is effective because it provides an instant and recognizable visual representation of the Vietnam War, without context or further explanation. In other words, it is ideally suited to the televisual news environment. Furthermore, the Baghdad nightscape images that follow contrast the Gulf War as seen from a distance in the night sky with the antithesis

Opening commentary:
Jackie Judd (Reporter): It was more than a year after America went to war in Vietnam that the nation began to stir. More than two years for the anti-war movement to really take shape. Now
»»»»»»»»»»»»»»»»»»»
fast-forward to 1991, the Persian Gulf War was only a few hours old when demonstrators hit the streets. In fact the protest movement began organizing for this day months earlier.

Closing commentary:
Judd: President Bush has not antagonized the protestors as Richard Nixon and Spirew Agnew once did. In fact, Mr Bush seems to go out of his way not to. One protest veteran says: a politician these days would be a fool to ignore the possibility that one day this background noise might turn into a deafening chorus of dissent. This is Jackie Judd for *Nightline* in Washington.

Figure 2 Extract from report on ABC News *Special Report: The Gulf War*, 18 January 1991

of the media's view of Vietnam, notably a 'close-up' war on the ground. So, through integrating templates into their coverage the US networks reinforced a simplistic and very limited snapshot memory of Vietnam.

The perception of the successful conclusion to the Gulf War enabled an apparently more definitive contrast to be made with the failures in Vietnam by the US media. For example, in a documentary produced for home video later in 1991 entitled *Desert Storm: The Victory* (Turner Home Entertainment), CNN used black-and-white footage of wounded soldiers in Vietnam evidently in some agony from their injuries. Outside of the real-time loop of this event, the war could more easily be depicted as 'not another Vietnam'. Moreover, the perception of the successful execution of the war enabled the American media to explicitly revisit Vietnam within a revised historical frame of military power in Bush's 'new world order'.

MEDIA TEMPLATES – 1991 TO 2003

In the same way that media coverage of the 1991 war drew upon living memory of the Vietnam War, the Iraq War had a more obvious, larger and much more recent constituency to shape its reporting – notably that of the Gulf War. One of the biggest news stories of 1991 was the capturing of Coalition pilots and their mistreatment and parading on television by Iraq. In 2003, the 1991 POWs were in great demand by the news networks for their authoritative take on the experience of being an Iraqi POW, particularly when five US soldiers were captured and paraded on Iraqi TV (along with bodies of dead Americans). John Nichol, an RAF navigator held in 1991, has since made a living from several books and from frequent TV appearances as a commentator on events in the region. For example, following renewed US air attacks on Iraq in 1996, Nichol appeared on a TV news programme which also aired 1991 images of him as a POW (BBC1 *9 O'Clock News*, 12 September 1996).

On 24 March 2003, Nichol's article describing his impressions of the 'ordeal facing US prisoners-of-war' was printed in the British (anti-war) *Daily Mirror* (Figure 3). The article incorporates an image of the 1991 Nichol as a visual template to frame the story and an image of one of the 2003 POWs, both from footage first broadcast on Iraqi television. He writes, 'The sheer terror etched on to their faces brought back a stream of horrific memories from when I went through the same thing during the first Gulf War . . . if Saddam Hussein thinks it will help him win the propaganda war, he could not be more wrong. These images will have the opposite effect.'

The personal account provided by Nichol conveys a certain (and as the byline claims exclusive) authority to comment on this story and con-jecture on its likely outcomes. Co-present survivors of warfare and other catastrophic events are often singled out by the news media and treated symbolically as representative of a particular experience or outcome. In this example, the archival memory of the media is mixed with the present-day human testimony of Nichol which provides a powerfully legitimizing frame to the story – claiming that the use of these images will backfire on the Iraqis (the previous page in the *Mirror*[19] carried six larger images of the captured and dead Americans appearing on Iraqi television and re-broadcast on Al-Jazeera TV). Other newspapers employed similar template devices; both the *Sun* and the *Daily Express* of 24 March, for example, used images of Nichol and another POW – John Peters – from the Gulf War, the *Express* making the comparison more explicitly in its headline: 'Evil Echoes of 1991'.

Human eyewitness memory and visual media connect and re-connect in influential ways to construct definitive and historical accounts of the past and to make sense of present events through those accounts. New memory of warfare involves an uneasy relationship between the static

Figure 3 Use of visual template in the press, page 4 of the *Daily Mirror*, 24 March 2003

and fixed video images of the past endlessly recycled in the present, and the dynamics and forgetfulness of human memory. And, when those who comment on events in the production of news today are inseparable from the *history* of the story, then alternative readings of events become more difficult to obtain, outside of the new mediated templates of memory.

During the build-up to the Iraq War, however, often catastrophic images from 1991 and earlier were employed as media frames. These are potentially most influential in this period, when public debate as to the merits and legitimacy of the impending attacks on Iraq was intensively documented in the British media. In the days and weeks before the start of the 2003 war, for example, BBC2's *Newsnight* correspondent Robin Denselow reported from Northern Iraq on the plight of the Kurds who had suffered over many years at the hands of Saddam Hussein's regime. In March, Denselow is in Chamchamal and files a report which centres around that week's fifteenth anniversary of Saddam's chemical attack on the town of Halabja. He narrates the events of 1988 over footage from the time of smoke rising from the town and two stills showing Kurdish civilian bodies strewn across the ground where they fell, including women and children. The report then shows a group of locals in the present watching a video documentary of the attack and an injured survivor recalls her experience (via a translator). (See Figure 4.)

This report combines the personal account of one of the victims and other Kurds also witness to the chemical attack on Halabja and its consequences with archive video material. The fact that a group of Kurds are also watching a video of this event is perhaps extraordinary. However, the report powerfully interweaves human memory with BBC archive material to produce an effective 'warning from history' of the possibility of the Kurds again suffering at the hands of Saddam, this

Denselow: This was Halabja 15 years ago. Saddam's chemicals killed 5,000 and injured another 10,000 – that's a third of those who lived here . . .

Rokhosh Mohammed (Survivor): All I remember is becoming blind. They took me to hospital in Iran. When I came back I couldn't find my family, all of them were dead – my parents, my brothers, my uncles, my cousins – all dead.

Denselow: The people of Halabja had no help then, and, for the moment at least, they have no help now. Though they are still under attack.

Figure 4   Extract from *Newsnight*, BBC2, 18 March 2003

time under the cover of the Iraq War. Again, the focus on the real horror of Halabja – the dead civilian women and children – is captured with the use of photographic images in the two stills inserted into the video report. The use of the still image in television is effective because it halts the flow of the medium and forces the viewer to linger, in this case for a few seconds on each still, which in televisual terms is a relatively long time to watch a frame without any movement in it or around it. The more routine visual procession of TV news both disguises and discards the single image at least in the moment, as Sontag argues: 'Image-flow precludes a privileged image' (2003: 106). The Kurdish bodies in this way become the central – and memorable – element in this report. The photographic – and so evidential – quality of these images also conveys more in terms of their function in documenting the terrible actions of Saddam Hussein. The still image captures more of the past, of history, as it appears removed from the essential movement and therefore ephemeral presentness of television.

Moreover, the media template of Halabja employed in the *Newsnight* programme functions to document simultaneously the brutal regime of Saddam *and* the consequences of inaction by the West to protect the Kurds in 1988 and 1991. Templates, in making connections between past experience and events in the present or likely future, construct powerful historical trajectories which frame ways of seeing. These accounts are very difficult to dispute in their chronology of events constructed through personal and visual media memory. And, in the build-up to the 2003 war, some of the British media at least produced a very different retrospective framing of the Gulf War – and one that was certainly not palatable to audiences of the time.

For example, on 14 February 2003, the *Guardian* newspaper devoted the whole of the *G2* section to 'The unseen Gulf war'. This was edited and introduced by the war photographer Don McCullin and contained mostly unpublished photographs that according to the section cover 'reveal the true horror of the Gulf war', along with accounts from journalists who had reported at the time. Most of the photographs show injured or dead Iraqis – soldiers and civilians – with the collection focusing on scenes on the road to Basra out of Kuwait on which retreating Iraqi troops were bombed and destroyed by Coalition forces at the end of the war.

Given that most of the images had not been previously published, this was in effect a new memory of the Gulf War in print (although a scene of an Iraqi soldier burned to death on the road to Basra, photographed by Ken Jarecke, has entered into the social memory of the war[20]). The *Guardian's* publication of graphic and disturbing photographs deliberately challenges the mediated social memory of a highly sanitized war of 1991 and, at the same time, indicts the media's role in perpetuating this notion through pampering audiences' sensibilities. The main critique assembled through the accounts of photographers and journalists in this newspaper, however, is the Pentagon and the system of reporting that prevented horrific scenes of some of those killed in 1991 from being reported at the time. These contrast the role of the (independent) photographer and journalist as witness and as documenter of the 'real' Gulf War against the contrived and highly sanitized version produced through pool reporting. They demonstrate (by their long-standing omission) just how effectively the media-managed images of 1991 have been retained in the collective memory of the war.

The *Guardian* publication of 14 February can be seen as a pre-emptive template of the Iraq War, as it was unlikely that such images would either be obtainable during the imminent conflict, or that readers would find them acceptable during the event time of war, if published. In other words, images of this nature would be perceived as unpatriotic by audiences who tend to be supportive of national military forces when in action even if they are unconvinced of the need for that action.

The actual role and impact of templates and the personal testimony of journalists and other observers, however, has not been adequately explored in terms of the images of warfare that they produce and reproduce. By 2003, the defining televisual images of the fireworks and video of precision strikes of 1991 had become obscured, at least in the British media, by the use of much more critical visual, and often photographic, templates. It was against this context – of the effective historical *revisioning* of the Gulf War through the work of mostly independent journalists – that the Pentagon forged their approach to the media in the Iraq War. For, in 2003, the Bush post-September 11 motif of being 'either with us or against us' was to encompass a new challenge beyond that of political or military support.

Chapter 3

Reality TV – war in real-time

NO-TIME NEWS

I have so far explored some of the 'ways of seeing' of the modern media and speculated as to how these might translate into our comprehension and memory of warfare over time. The relationship between the journalist, the means or technology of news-gathering and dissemination, and the event being reported as 'news', however, has been the subject of considerable debate. For instance, how do journalists routinely sift and select from incoming comparatively 'raw' material? Why is one image chosen and used over another?

How events come to be defined as 'news' in the first place is part of a long-standing debate, or rather assumption, about the criteria that effect journalistic selections and reselections, in other words the existence of 'news values' or 'newsworthiness'.[21] The increased mobility of journalists and their enhanced capacity to report in real time from or near to the event they are covering have become more and more influential. Indeed, the reduction in time between an event occurring and its public dissemination is fundamental in shaping the content of news today. Whilst 'time is the scaffolding on which [news] stories are hung' (Schudson, 1987: 97), television as *the* medium of time (Hoskins, 2001a: 213) is simply able to deliver stories and images more immediately to mass audiences than any other medium, and so dominates the communication of contemporary events.

Although some media theorists acknowledge the impact of 'timeliness' or 'immediacy' on news values (e.g. see Allan, 1999), most still cling to an outdated list which remains the outmoded fare of rather tired Schools of Journalism and Media Studies in the UK, USA and elsewhere.[22] At the same time, there have also been a number of scholars (and some journalists, notably Nik Gowing) who have investigated the impact of real-time images on politicians, governments, etc. In times of war and other catastrophes, time is of more consequence than in the coverage of other events, as audience responses to real-time images, and the action or inaction of politicians and military leaders in turn, may save or end lives. So, the impact of the immediacy of television has been taken very seriously, with numerous studies identifying the medium's *reflexivity*, that is to say, its ability to feed into and shape the event being covered by news programming – the so-called 'CNN effect' (Boden and Hoskins, 1995; Livingston, 1997; Volkmer, 1999; Robinson, 2002). In recent years especially, television has entered into the actual production of the events it records, in that process altering the moment-by-moment trajectory of events. In this way, the medium is not only the message but also enters into the constitution of society itself.

At the same time, the compulsion for live and on-location reporting is indicted for a 'dumbing down' of news content. Jon Swain (2003: 29), for example, claims:

> Television has become a 24-hour slog with the result that while many of today's TV reporters may have all the traditional dedication and intrepidness of their predecessors, they cannot use it. They are tied to the satellite dish on the hotel roof ready to deliver 'live spots' and so are unable to explore in depth the stories they are supposed to be reporting.

In this way a drive for immediacy directly constrains the ability of journalists to perform their jobs effectively.

Furthermore, to thoroughly verify the accuracy and sources of the rapid flow of information and rumour would considerably slow the news-flow, to the advantage of one's competitors. This makes news networks more vulnerable to the breaking of inaccurate stories, as Mark Lawson (2003a) argues, 'the Iraq war has emphasised the primary disadvantage of live journalism: that reporting often benefits from checks and second thoughts'.[23] This chapter considers these contradictions in no-time news and explores the function of liveness in constructing news in a format that resembles so-called 'reality television', notably a genre of entertainment programming.

The Gulf War was a comparatively 'slow' affair. Whereas the 2003 war provided lots of reality television – real soldiers in a real war in real time

– most of this was actually 'down time', that is time between engagements with an enemy. But this is the reality of warfare – Iraq War coverage could never hope to deliver the expectations generated by other live
programme formats that have proliferated post-1991. After all, tune into
a *Big Brother* household on a 24-hour basis and continuous action and
interest is not sustainable. The increasingly task-driven nature of this TV
format is an attempt to provide structure and guaranteed interaction
between contestants at peak times; live (or almost-live) television coverage of house-mates sitting around or sleeping does not hold audiences
for very long. Television news teams do not have the luxury of staging
events (although the US military were quite obliging in 2003, and
famously with the 'toppling' of the statue of Saddam Hussein in
Baghdad).

Instead, a 'flooding' of the present is achieved partly through the use
of videographics, but partly through the increased deployment of
simultaneity. That is to say, a multitude of live cameras (as in the *Big
Brother* household) enables a constant switching between locations and
events (or non-events) and often the simultaneous broadcast of different locations, in different windows within the television screen. This
was a feature of both Gulf Wars, although split-screen views tended to
consist more of talking heads in 1991 than in 2003, when there were
simply more news networks, more cameras, and thus more alternative
shots. However, unlike the panoptic views afforded by television at
sporting events where few moves go unseen, extending this model of
coverage from the football field to the battlefield actually produces a
highly distorted vision. The experience of 'being there' as a television
witness to an unfolding news event is similar, but the apparent ubiquity
of vision created through reporting from multiple locations at the same
time can afford the impression of an unmediated view. Whereas 1991
coverage depended upon an extended *discourse* of liveness to maintain
the continuity of the event – the sense that *something* was always occurring or about to occur – the Iraq War was easier for broadcasters in that
frequently a reporter on-location, or in the studio, could just stand
back and say 'look at this'. In this way, the threshold for what was
included in continuous coverage was lowered, as long as it was happening live, on-location, and preferably in Iraq. In this way, the significance
of the content of news diminishes as the demand for immediacy
increases.

The liveness of TV news can be said to 'cover up' the discontinuities of the television event, through its pace, urgency and simultaneity, as though real-time coverage was not a fast enough mode of dissemination. Sean Cubitt (1991: 36), for example, argues that 'Liveness in a sense serves to mask the fragmentary nature of television.' Televisual news narrative of an event is displaced by more urgent information and images. The immediacy of no-time news carries with it that which Mary Ann Doane (1990: 224) calls 'the automatic truth value'. There is simply something more convincing about watching an event happening as it is being broadcast than watching something that has been re-packaged as a recorded film report. And liveness is further facilitated by the live and direct mode of contact of the news anchor, who bridges presence and absence; television events carry with them a familiarity of the persistent and the personal, a mode of dissemination that easily resonates with the everyday conscious. Audiences are routinely welcomed into the shared presence of the news anchor, who provides concern and reassurance through vicarious eye-contact with the viewer.

The news discourse of liveness that really emerged much more self-consciously during 1991 served to disguise the fact that very little genuinely 'new' information was available to news networks. This was hardly reality television but, rather, more closely resembled that which Adam (1990: 140–1) describes as a process of 'innovation, repetition and discarding'.[24]

However, despite these constructions of real-time news – or because of them – the appetite and demand for liveness in television appears to have increased over time. If one compares the amount of live-on-location material broadcast, for example, in 1991 and 2003, it is the latter that at least appeared to have more and certainly that has become a defining feature of the war for many commentators. If one goes back and checks one's own memory of the TV coverage from 1991, it is apparent how comparatively *slow* this reporting is. The 2003 war ushered in a much faster pace of event time and an apparent closeness – or even intimacy – with the war and those involved in it. Intense competition and audience expectations have become driven by a compulsion for reality television in the form of reporters embedded in amongst the events they are reporting on and these being watched by audiences unfolding in real time on TV screens. Martin Bell (2003), for example, argues that in their coverage of the Iraq War Sky Television was reduced to 'Breaking

Rumour' rather than 'Breaking News'. The pressure to broadcast unverified – and thus potentially inaccurate – reports reached new heights in this environment. More than any previous conflict, 'Breaking News' during the Iraq War became mostly an overused front for vacuous and/or unverified content. The capacity of television reporting to deliver continuously live on-location images involves the medium outpacing the message. There is simply not enough 'new' or reliable information to sustain continuous televisual coverage of wars and other catastrophes for very long at the pace at which a culture of instant gratification demands. However, once resources are committed, networks are obliged to maintain a certain level of coverage, particularly when others are providing a service around-the-clock. This has led to a growing reality gap between the occasional actuality footage of genuine newsworthiness, and an increasingly contrived and shallow discourse covering for an absence of hard news.

Here, I explore these contradictions in changing news environments and consider some of the potential consequences for longer-term comprehension and memory of events when originally screened as no-time news. In this way I identify changing modes of war as 'television event', first capturing the imagination of audiences in the forced temporalities and relatively singular CNN vision of the Gulf War, through to today's saturating multi-network world of no-time news.

1991 – NEW TIMES AND PLACES

Something is happening outside . . .

(Bernard Shaw, CNN live, 16 January 1991)

This statement uttered on the first night of the Gulf War by one of the US network's three correspondents in a hotel room in the al-Rashid Hotel, Baghdad, unwittingly expressed the global televisual phenomenon of which the speaker was an instrument. 'Outside' did not merely include the potential danger that lay beyond the hotel room door, that is from the danger of discovery by Iraqi security undertaking 'sweeps' of the hotel (predominantly home to foreign journalists) to ensure residents were safely (and securely) in the basement air raid shelter. Rather, the satellite feed carried the correspondents' live commentary via CNN to a global audience, rendering the hotel room door somewhat transparent. What Bernard Shaw did not grasp in this moment of live broadcast was that the global space of the audience he was addressing also included the Iraqis themselves. They presumably were in a position to communicate with hotel security at the al-Rashid. The CNN reporters even remarked on the elaborate bluff one of their number – Peter Arnett – pulled off in claiming to be too frightened to go down to the basement shelter with the other journalists after his 'experience of bombing raids in Vietnam', during a visit from hotel security staff. It only later became apparent to them that their continued presence and reporting live was no accident but could have been halted by either the Iraqis or the Americans at any moment. Their *presence* was 'extended' electronically beyond a local form, that of their immediate surroundings, out into the global. And yet, they were also *part of* a global space constituent of the news event – the Gulf War – affected by their very reporting. In this way, instantaneous communication created a reflexive loop in global space and across global times to potentially shape the news event being communicated.

One of the compelling features for audiences watching in 1991 was that this was the first war that appeared 'live' – unfolding on the screen in 'real time'. Liveness (although here I focus on its construction by newsworkers) is a phenomenon that has been observed as a property of the medium – as something intrinsic to television itself – making it different from other mediums. The work of McLuhan is central in this respect. He argues that, 'The elementary and basic fact about the TV image is that it is a mosaic or a mesh, continuously in a state of formation by the "scanning finger". Such a mosaic involves the viewer in a perpetual act of participation and completion' (1962, 1987: 286–7). The 'tactile' nature of the televisual experience for McLuhan can be said to be part of the 'ontological' make-up of television. However, liveness is much more than this. Recognition of the attractions of the live 'experience' has led to its appropriation by television news and other media, and today it is highly constructed through news scripts, broadcast talk, and a whole range of visual cues and videographics (see, for example, Feuer, 1983; Marriott, 1995; Hoskins, 2001a).

Liveness was a dominant feature of the television reporting of the Gulf War. Reporters often provided dramatic pieces to camera by focusing upon 'their' position in relation to events around them and upon the potential danger they themselves were in. For example, on 18 January

1991, Charles Jaco is reporting live for CNN from 'somewhere near an airbase' at night in Saudi Arabia:

> Yes here in Dhahran – here in Eastern Saudi Arabia an air raid is on, we have reports of five Scud missiles in the air. There have been explosions around here as Patriot missiles have streaked into the air behind us. Air raid sirens are going off all over the city, we're being told to abandon this position immediately. But some sort of air raid is going on. We do have reports of five Scud missiles incoming, we don't know if they're true. We do know that Patriot ground-to-air missiles are being fired. Everyone is being told to scramble, off this platform, right now, uh we're trying to see what's gonna happen but as of right now, we have reports of five Patriot – er five Scud missiles coming in toward us.

In this piece of reporting, Jaco is standing on a wooden platform with a panoramic perspective of nothing more than the darkness of night and a few lights on the horizon. Throughout he turns around nervously peering into darkness and only looks into the camera occasionally, clutching a clip-on microphone, which presumably he has not had time to attach.

Jaco's talk revolves around mostly present-tense expressions (e.g. 'an air raid is on', 'we have reports' and 'everyone is being told', etc.), and so might be said to be typical of the live television reporting that has developed since. Marriott, for example, argues, 'Live television commentary typically involves . . . an "experiential" mode of description, which is used to talk about events or processes that are occurring at or around the moment of utterance (with events presented either as if they have just occurred or as if they are occurring now)' (1995: 351). In the extract above, Jaco latches onto anything and everything that obtains in the moment: most convenient in this instance are the air raid sirens. Often networks went live to locations whenever sirens were sounding as they conveyed immediacy and urgency to reports. With similar effect, the darkness, the sky and the streets beyond, are all elements that are employed to anchor the commentary in the 'here and now' in this report, with Jaco gesticulating out into the night. In fact, Jaco uses the expression *right now* eleven times in his full report.

These elements relate fundamentally to the relationship of time to the production and dissemination of news stories. News by its very nature is limited by time, its whole currency and value depends upon its recency.

George Steiner (1991: 27), for example, argues, 'Journalistic presentation generates a temporality of equivalent instantaneity. All things are more or less of equal import; all are only daily. Correspondingly, the content, the possible significance of the material which journalism communicates, is "remaindered" the day after.' In the competitive world of broadcast journalism in recent years there has developed a more aggressive signification of time; news reporters and anchors tend to cling to their temporal currency obsessively, almost as though real-time reporting were a charade that disguises an absence of 'hard news' beneath. In television news today, there appears an increasing conflation of the reporting of an event (this is happening) and information relating to the time and place of its reporting (this is being brought to you here-and-now).

A key feature of Jaco's live reporting is its disfluency. The 'uhms', 'ers' and recyled phrases as he tries to react and comment in real time were characteristic of much of the live-on-location broadcast talk. This live bumbling about on desert rooftops and outside airbases was actually part of the CNN effect and part of the televisual quality of the war that hooked and addicted viewers to the often simulated liveness of a new television experience.

In addition to an overwhelming focus by reporters on the present, broadcast talk is also obsessed with the future. Television news attempts to hold viewers through the perpetual promise of events yet to come. This is particularly the case during continuous coverage of major news events. News programme anchors in particular are sellers of future time. This is evident in their use of language, which is dominated by references to events of the future as well as the present; viewers are constantly pulled forward into the next moment by the *deixis* employed by the speaker. A useful way to consider the future-tensed phenomenon of broadcast talk is with reference to Helga Nowotny's idea of an 'extended present'. For example, as Adam argues, 'This suggests a porosity and permeability of the boundary between the present and the future, a blurring that makes it impossible to establish which time dimension we are dealing with' (1990: 141).

Of course there was some genuine confusion amongst global audiences, with coverage of the Gulf War geared around the different time zones of Atlanta, Baghdad, and Tel Aviv, for example. Night and day merged in the round-the-clock coverage, audiences watching CNN (or their own national networks carrying CNN feeds) were immersed in a time-cycle that seemed out-of-sync. It is no wonder that many commentators have referred to this viewing experience as 'unreal', a point not lost on the journalists themselves. Bernard Shaw in Baghdad, for example, reflects on his experience of reporting the first night of the war, 'There is one sound I will never get out of my mind of this experience . . . that was hearing . . . that rooster crowing yet still pitch black and the bombs are falling.' Meanwhile, it was the role of the news anchors to attempt to stitch the multiple times and places together into some continuity of coverage, although it was the *dis*continuities of jumping from different times and places that often added to the immediate viewing experience.

To what extent liveness is constructed through broadcast talk, icons and other visual gimmicks, or driven by the pace and locations of the event being covered as news itself, is a complex question. A lot of the liveness of CNN's coverage was 'accidental', in the sense that the initial al-Rashid Hotel reporting owed a great deal to journalists being in the right place at the right time. However, what is apparent is that CNN soon recognized the success of these features and increasingly embellished and dwelled upon them.

One means of assessing the use and effects of time in news broadcasts is through examination of the language and structure of reporting. Unlike personal story-telling, news stories are rarely told in the order that events happened. Allan Bell (1998: 96), for example, with reference to a printed piece of news observes, 'In the body of the story, perceived *news value* overturns temporal sequence and imposes an order completely at odds with linear narrative' (italics in original). In other words news components or items deemed more newsworthy, particularly in relation to those occurring most recently, tend to appear first. Bell uses this feature to develop a framework for analysing the time structure of a published piece of news text. In this he defines 'time zero' as the 'story present', which is the time of the first event in the first sentence of his selected news report. The event referred to which occurred in time immediately preceding the day/date of the story (time zero), Bell codes '-1', and the event prior to this as '-2', and so on. Similarly, events referred to in future time receive a positive number, according to their chronological position after time zero. Bell uses this framework to show how events are represented in news stories to enhance their recency. For example, the most recent event (or most recent developments in an ongoing story) is often placed first, at the expense of chronological order. In this way, the news values of recency or immediacy overturn linear narrative and temporal sequence. So, according to Bell, news stories are often written with a 'corkscrew' structure that refers to the way in which narrative moves backwards and forwards in time.

In broadcast talk, however, the present tense is embodied in the talk of the reporter or anchor; time zero is constant with live commentary narration as it exists with reference to the unfolding moments of speech. In the study of linguistics, the use of words relating to the time and place of utterance is known as deixis. And the deictics of news talk are fundamental to constructing a shared here-and-now of speaker and viewer; the discourse of presenters and journalists attempt to carry audiences with them literally into the place and time, event and story. For example, use of the future tense and references to events in the future function to extend the present, constantly reminding viewers why they should stay with the programme. To provide one example, it is crucially the opening of the war on CNN that set a temporal standard for other news networks as well as for its own later coverage. Taken from this period is an extract of the talk of CNN's Washington anchor, David French (Figure 5), as he struggles to provide some kind of continuity between two live, on-location reports, one from the al-Rashid in Baghdad and one geographically much closer to home, from Virginia.

One relatively easy way of achieving an ongoing sense of liveness is through reference in news language to time itself and to the time of events. In the ensuing transcript, the news anchor multi-references time in his live commentary. I have provided line numbers to this transcript, and in Table 2, I have adapted Bell's form of time analysis and applied this to the anchor's talk.

Figure 5 Transcript of David French, anchor, CNN Washington Studio, 5.00 a.m. Baghdad time. 16 January 1991 (length of segment: 33 seconds)

1 Compelling reporting gentlemen, thank you very much –
2 it's coming up on Wve o'clock in the morning in Baghdad
3 and behind that, not too far, will be light.
4 President Bush is going to address the nation er shortly
5 within er twelve or thirteen minutes. And er
6 the lull that their talking about
7 having lasted twenty-Wve minutes. May well er continue er

8 until that is over.
9 Also we're expecting er a brieWng er from the Secretary of Defence
10 and er Joint Chiefs Chairman Colin Powell at the Pentagon,
11 following the President's remarks.
12 Now let's go to Norfolk, Virginia . . .

Table 2: Time expressions in CNN transcript

Line no.	Story Time Baghdad/EST	Time Expression
2	0	it's coming up on
2	+1	five o'clock in the morning
3	+2	behind that, not too far,
3	+2	will be light
4	+1	going to
4	+1	shortly
5	+1	within . . . twelve or thirteen minutes
6	−1	lull
7	−2	lasted twenty-five minutes
8	+2? +2	until that is over
11	+2	following the President's remarks
12	0	Now

There are obvious differences between a pre-structured piece of printed news and the unfolding instantaneous commentary of the passage above, although a similar corkscrew patterning of references to times can be identified. More significant, however, is that deictic references to future time and to time zero in this extract together outnumber past references by a ratio of 5:1. Most of this talk directs the viewer into the extended present of the war, to future events.

Clearly, in the mostly unscripted commentary on live events, comprehension is not comparable to the standard of a written and pre-edited text. The employment of multiple times of reference evident in the transcript above provides a constantly shifting temporal positioning. The corkscrew effect, however, is not an easy commentary to follow. In line 1, for example, 'it's coming up on' can be read as 'it's *almost* . . .'. And, in line 3, 'and behind that, not too far, will be light' perhaps is more comprehensible as '*after* that, not too *long* after, it will be light'. So, the anchor is using expressions characteristic of that which Marriott (above) terms the experiential mode of description. Rather than using more usual temporal adverbs, line 3 is characterized by spatial expressions. This promotes the here-and-now of the anchor, commentating as if he were also in Baghdad, and sharing this temporal space/place with viewers.

If we return to the live-on-location extract of Charles Jaco (above) and compare it with the David French studio narrative, the temporal differences in the story time are evident. Table 3 refers to the Jaco reporting, in which the most obvious expressions of time and tense are underlined and spatial expressions are italicized.

Table 3: Expressions of time, tense and space taken from a transcript of Charles Jaco reporting from Saudi Arabia as part of a CNN live link with Atlanta, 18 January 1991

Line no.	Story Time	Expressions of time, tense and space
5–6	0	*here* in Dhahran – *here* in Eastern Saudi Arabia
6	0	an air raid is on
7–8	−1	There have been explosions around *here*
8–10	−1	missiles have streaked
10	0	into the air *behind us*
10–11	0	sirens are going off
11	0	we're being told
11–12	0	to abandon *this position* immediately
12–13	0	air raid is going on
13	0	We do have
13	0	we don't know
14	0	we do know
15	0	missiles are being fired
15–16	0	being told to scramble
16	0	o:ff *this platform*, right now
17	0	as of right now
18	0	we have reports
19	0	coming in *toward us*
→ Anchor question		
22	0	We have a shelter and we have gas masks
28	0	right now
28	−1	we've had
29	−1	past few minutes
29	−1	we've been told
30	0	Scuds are incoming
30	−1	we've heard
31	−1	seen the *streets behind us*
31–32	−1	missiles have gone up

In a sense one can identify an iterative loop within the report from Dhahran itself. There is very little new information provided, of any consequence, after the first twenty lines. Indeed, the main components are established within this opening segment of Jaco's report, namely the location, the facts that it is night-time and that incoming Scud missiles are being met with a Patriot missile defence response, the danger to Jaco and the fact that his crew are reporting despite having been told to leave their current platform position, and the fact that air raid sirens are being sounded. These facts are recycled for the duration of this report, which, with the focusing on the actual time of the speech itself, combine to produce quite a 'condensed' piece of reporting. Most of the '-1' clusters in the story time appear later, after the handover and question from the anchor, prompting some kind of update or review from Jaco in response. However, on each occasion the flow of the commentary is soon brought forward into the now of the speaker. Overall, these features of talk add to the intensity and the urgency of Jaco's position.

Although these are somewhat crude measures of liveness, the zeros evident in the news time of this example are indicative of a feature of television news that, although not new in 1991, helped set a new threshold for audience expectations. However, in his report, Jaco appears genuinely to believe that his position is about to come under attack from Scud missiles. The problem for news networks was that this was an exception to the rule. Notably, without any live actuality footage of combat, the mainstay of coverage was a mix of recorded pool footage, talking heads and journalists getting as close as they were allowed to the potential sites of conflict in the hope that they would be able to broadcast something (that is *any*thing) of the war in real time. Most of the time, however, they were reduced to reacting to *potential* threats to themselves, to the extent that journalists (and their presence in a war zone) became the story.

2003 – 'NEW PROPAGANDA' – VISIONS OF SPEED AND PROXIMITY

The Iraq War ushered in the videophone as the standard of television war reporting rather than the exception; visual immediacy ruled supreme. Over 600 journalists were embedded with the US dominated forces with almost 100 highly-mobile television cameras across the battlefield. (This compares with the apparently much tighter control of the pool reporting system imposed in the Gulf War when, at least initially, amongst over half a million troops distributed over a vast area of desert the Coalition permitted only twelve photographers.)

To draw a comparison with Vietnam, coverage of the Iraq War suffered from a saturation of sources and from being overfilmed, whereas the former was actually more staged than people remember because network camera crews had to rely on the military to transport their heavy equipment[25] and were censored by their relative immobility. Photographers were more mobile than network film units and simply had potentially easier and faster access to events. Nonetheless, as Arlen (1982: 75) argues, '. . . the Vietnam news was a crowded, overtalked, overfilmed, almost banal jumble, which was hugely difficult for people to relate to in any coherent fashion'. Although Arlen also acknowledges that audiences did eventually relate to the war, his description of Vietnam here is also applicable to coverage of events in and around Iraq in 2003.

The increased number of sources, a saturation of news outlets, and the speed of communications reaching those outlets direct from the war zone, combined to effect a frenzy of so-called breaking news. David Puttnam (2003: 50), for example, argues:

> 'Operation Iraqi Freedom' was a war fought live on television; the propaganda war was largely fought *through* television. In fact, it's probably something of a paradigm for the way mainstream journalism will increasingly operate in the modern era. It exemplified the manner in which a combination of technology, a culture of instant gratification and the commercial fragmentation of the media have conspired to shape news in modern times. (*original emphasis*)

The intensification of these pressures demonstrates how influential temporal factors have become in television news, particularly when compared with the comparatively slower drip, drip of information and news flow that in 1991 was marked by its immediacy. The combination of these influences, however, is difficult to separate out in terms of identifying single causes, but it is interesting to consider their intersection. For example, as I have suggested of no-time news, the Iraq War was mediated in a televisual environment quite different to that of 1991. Many commentators have argued that the consumption of popular culture in Western society has been marked by a shortening of temporal horizons and have critiqued audiences' diminishing attention-spans. Todd Gitlin, for example, even extends this critique to the consumption of popular American fiction. He equates falls in the average sentence length and the number of punctuation marks with the rise of television in national culture: 'popular fiction has gotten stripped down and now looks more like television. It goes down easier and makes fewer demands' (2001: 101).

A 'three-minute culture' is seen as driven increasingly by a demand of and for the moment, producing (or produced by) distracted channel-hopping audiences. Fashions, pop stars, hit movies, celebrities, etc. move in and out of extreme exposure almost overnight. Reality- (and often real-time-) based and other entertainment television programmes, for example, have been successfully constructed upon this premise, e.g. *Big Brother* and *Pop Idol*, where instant celebrity is the format's promise and guarantor. Reality television has become a metaphor for the idea that what viewers are watching is largely unscripted, and driven by events that unfold in real time. In this environment, television news involving lengthy, detailed and retrospective analysis has little chance of attracting mass audiences.

However, in 2003, news networks got closer to the reality TV format than ever before, as journalists themselves became contestants in warfare. And news packaged as entertainment provided the requisite celebratization of participants (the BBC's Rageh Omar and CNN's Walter Rodgers, for example). Networks succumbed to the entertainment format of reality television as news values were collapsed into the need for events of the moment. If a given network didn't have live pictures then it would take a feed from one that did. Alternatively, television would simply provide simultaneous views, with the extended use of split-frames and multiple windows on screen. In this way, the networks attempted to mimic the effects of the remote control, negating the temptation of the viewer to switch channel. The result was a running perspective on the war that did not provide a coherent picture. Mark Lawson (2003b), for example, argues, 'Because we must always doubt the meaning of the scenes we're seeing, following this war on television is like walking around an art gallery in which the pictures dissolve and the captions scramble shortly after you've been admiring them for 20 minutes.' The impatience of event time coverage does not allow pause for focus, because the next moment is always more important. The exception is the capture of an iconic image, which is (conversely) repeated and dissected until it loses all context and meaning, other than it being recognizable *as* an iconic image: the dramatic, or rather dramatized, rescue of the POW Private Jessica Lynch is one example.

EMBEDS AT WAR

In the meantime, and between iconic images, the sheer number of embedded journalists in the field enabled greater simultaneity than ever before, delivering a continuous feed of live material from the zone of conflict. On occasion, the 'embeds', as they became known, produced vivid and dramatic images, although mostly they provided highly personalized accounts reflecting the experiences of the soldiers they travelled and lived amongst. Embeds travelling on convoys, for example, driving along Iraqi highways, afforded at least a sense of pace, speed, and movement. This was strangely compelling viewing, sometimes with the embeds riding alongside military vehicles, attempting to provide live commentary as they were bounced around with the Iraqi countryside speeding by. This included using low-angle shots with the camera positioned near to wheel-level to construct the convoy as larger-than-life. There was a real sense of purpose and destination conveyed in these literally rolling live broadcasts, somewhat reminiscent of road movies, with the adventure and camaraderie of travel on the open highway. Moreover, it was the occasional plume of smoke or passing twisted wreckage that offered mere diversions, as the central characters in this movie were the embeds themselves. It was their journey and their story.

However, the journalists closest to the heart of battle itself ironically contributed mostly narrow and decontextualized snapshots of the war. Moreover, the shrinking of the physical distance between embed and soldier was matched by a shrinking of the critical distance between journalist and story. In effect the Americans had successfully planted spokesmen and women for the Pentagon all over the battlefield. This was a triumph not lost on the American administration. For example, speaking on Fox TV (the most cheerleading of the war of all news networks), Bryan Whitman, the Deputy Assistant Secretary of Defence with responsibility for the embed programme, spoke of its success:

The American people won because they got to see exactly how well-trained, how well-equipped and how well-led their US military is . . . One of the reasons why we did this was to counter dis-information out there, to counter Saddam's lies. You know it was Greg Kelly [Fox TV embed] as he was rolling through the streets of Baghdad and you still had the Minister of Information saying no we have defeated the US forces, we have repelled the US forces, no there's no Americans here in Baghdad. So it was that type of thing where Greg Kelly right there in Baghdad was able to counter that kind of dis-information by being there and reporting objectively right from the battlefield. (*Fox News, live, 16 April 2003*)

This unprecedented contact between the media and the military carried with it an intense debate as to diminishing prospects for objective and detached reporting, as hinted at by Whitman above in his claim of objectivity in Fox News' coverage. Embeds actually lived with the story they were reporting on and were utterly dependent upon the military for their field of vision and whole capacity to report, not to mention their safety. The timing of their reports followed military cycles and priorities and not news cycles. For example, NBC's correspondent Chip Reid with the US First Marine Division even reported in a very quiet voice to avoid disturbing the rest of those he was embedded with: 'forgive me for speaking very quietly but I am in a field of sleeping marines right now, it was a very long day, they got up well before dawn this morning and have spent the entire day moving north' (MSNBC, live, 23 March 2003).

The circumstances in which embedded journalists operated thus effectively closed down the opportunity for critical correspondence, as Jamie Wilson (2003: 5) reporting from the HMS *Marlborough* points out: 'It is undoubtedly much harder for journalists to be impartial when they are living with and have grown to like the people they are writing about. They treated me well and I guess that was always in the back of my mind when I was writing about them.' Embeds were hardly likely to report, 'the soldiers I'm living with are bored and exhausted. They can't see any justification for this war. They're worried about shooting at their own side, and they're probably not all going to make it.' Living with a story simply does not afford time or space for open and critical journalism.

However, the intersection of the media and military which marked the Iraq War also appeared in more institutionalized forms, as veterans of armed service were increasingly employed as TV pundits. There was an obvious constituency of former military 'experts' to draw upon, some of whom had previously been the subject of 1991 television war reporting themselves. For example, General Barry McCaffrey, commander of the 24th Infantry Division during the Gulf War, was employed by NBC, and former NATO supreme commander during the 1999 War over Kosovo, General Wesley Clark, has worked for CNN for some time.

Fox News employed the notorious White House aide-turned-radio-talk-show-host Colonel Oliver North, who was actually embedded as a journalist with the US 1st Marine Expeditionary Force in Iraq. Unsurprisingly, North's reporting resonated with the conversational and decidedly patriotic discourse of Fox. For example, the following exchange between the studio anchor and North in southern Iraq seems inappropriate given the gravity and potential dangers of warfare on which they are reporting:

Anchor: One of our good guys is Oliver North and he's embedded with the 1st Marine Expeditionary Force and we go to him live right now. Good morning!

North: Lauren, how are you today? It's a beautiful day here on the outskirts of Tikrit. (*Fox News, live, 12 April 2003*)

Similarly, the following extract is typical of the almost frivolous exchanges between Fox News anchors as the embedded North reports from Iraq:

Anchor: And now joining us from somewhere in the Baghdad vicinity Lieutenant Colonel Oliver North U.S.M.C. retired and one of the Fox News embeds. Ollie, what's new?

North: Tony, as Rebecca Gonas just reported, elements of the 1st Marine Expeditionary Force on the way north as General Brooks briefed earlier today at the CentCom brief. Above me in this tactical assembly area a wonderful sky-lit night laced with the contrails of those aircraft that are still being [inaudible] even though the Abraham Lincoln may be headed home. And outside the perimeter right here a quieter night than we have had yet in Baghdad. Last night there was gunfire literally around the clock. Tonight, quiet. It started right after dark last night. Tonight the locals are trying to tell us where the quote – foreigners – are, the foreigners to them not the Americans but those who have come to support the regime of Saddam Hussein from other countries. And everywhere we go, Tony, literally everywhere: every school, every athletic facility, even in mosques, we find the ammunition of Saddam Hussein. He had to be the *Imelda Marcos* of grenades . . . Tony that's the latest from the 1st Marine Expeditionary Force.

Anchor: Ollie, thank you so much. The *Imelda Marcos* of grenades – what a line! (*Fox News, live, 12 April 2003*)

Table 4: Time expressions, Fox News, live, 12 April 2003

Story Time	Expressions of time, tense and space
−1	just reported
−1	on the way *north*
−1	briefed earlier today
0	*above me*
0	*in this tactical assembly area*
0	a wonderful *sky-lit night*
0	aircraft that are still being
0	may be headed
0	*outside the perimeter*
0	*right here*
0	A quieter night
−1	than we have had yet
0	*in Baghdad.*
−1	Last night there was gunfire
−1	Literally around the clock.
0	Tonight, quiet.
−1	It started right after dark last night.
0	Tonight

North's talk (Table 4) is very similar to Jaco's reporting (Table 3) in its experiential description of his situation, focusing upon the here-and-now with the story time of this piece dominated by the present (0) and the recent past (−1). However, this style and content of reporting was simply much more available in 2003 than in 1991, owing to the sheer number of journalists and embeds in the zone of conflict. This effect was similar to the reporting of the aftermath of September 11, 2001, when a number of news networks simply moved out of their New York studios and set up outside broadcasts with the smouldering city skyline as their backdrop. 'Being there' at the scene of a major event provides an inherent immediacy, bringing a visual liveness to news coverage that is increasingly expected by audiences fed a diet of reality TV programming elsewhere in their schedules.

AMERICAN VISIONS

In terms of the wider implications, North's reporting is typical of the general patriotic content and tone of Fox News' discourse on the war. This tended to swing between the exhilaration of battle and a kind of 'post-tourist' postcard depiction of the terrain and events, for example, the comments 'it's a beautiful day here' and 'a wonderful sky-lit night laced with the contrails of those aircraft', and a poking of fun at the enemy, '[Saddam] had to be the *Imelda Marcos* of grenades'.

Reporters working for the British media, however, were also literally swept along with the military units with which they were embedded. In addition to liberal use of the first-person plural, the discourse of the embeds often reflected the power of the military machines and the desert landscape through which they raced. In this way reports filed from the embedded 'travellers' became excessively cinematic in their description, evoking Hollywood, the Wild West (very much like the experience of travels through *America* that Jean Baudrillard describes[26]), and consequently contributed little to an understanding of the broader war. For example, Mark Franchetti writes in the *Sunday Times*,

> We were racing across the lunar landscape in attack formation, hundreds of vehicles trailing plumes of dust and bringing war . . . The roar of the engines was immense, a rolling thunder over the barren plains. To the occasional stunned shepherds, we invaders must have seemed like ghosts out of a Mad Max movie. (*7 April 2003*)

The individual experiential reports of the embeds fragmented coverage into hundreds of touristic diaries of adventure, travel and discovery.

Their accounts of the deadly realities of war often resembled the tone of *Lonely Planet* travel guides, as though viewers themselves might want to follow the same routes and observe the 'sets' for themselves. Coverage of the Iraq War blurred travel writing and news reporting into what John Urry has called the 'tourist gaze':

> part of that experience is to gaze upon or view a set of different scenes, of landscapes or townscapes which are out of the ordinary. When we 'go away' we look at the environment with interest and curiosity. It speaks to us in ways we appreciate or anticipate that it will do so. In other words, we gaze at what we encounter. (*2002: 1*)

Of course, in our contemporary age, the post-tourist can increasingly 'experience' the tourist gaze vicariously through television and new media. But the fundamental problem with the encroachment of 'news' into the realm of entertainment is, as I have suggested above, the loss of perspective on the awful consequences and cost of warfare.

The post-tourist embeds helped to mediate quite a different perspective of place compared with Gulf War television coverage. The simultaneous events around the Gulf and in the West of 1991 were brought together into both a single global present and presence by their televisual mediation. Joshua Meyrowitz, for example, claims that: 'By bringing many different people to the same "place", electronic media ... affect us not primarily through their content, but by changing the "situational geography" of social life' (1985: 6). 1991 marked a shift in the experience of time and place of many through the connecting of distant and disparate locations being fed through a single shared American news time and place (CNN usually being anchored from Atlanta, New York or Washington). Global audiences may have been transported to far-and-away places, and sometimes to several locations simultaneously, but they were always 'brought back' to the US. The 'situational geography' of the Gulf War was undoubtedly American.

Although many Western and other countries received their own national programming, most were reliant on CNN and other US network satellite feeds (as well as pool footage approved by the Pentagon). The French channel TF1, for example, regularly carried CBS from the States to which it added subtitles. The global picture of the Gulf War was powerfully framed from and by the USA and alternative perspectives to this view were difficult to find. McKenzie Wark (1994: 13), for example, writes of his frustration in this respect:

> It was difficult, as an Australian, not to experience the war as something that happened in America, performed, acted, and sponsored by Americans, for Americans. On television, most voices were American. All the images looked American. Even Saddam seemed to be an American.

The broadcasting landscape has transformed since 1991, with the fragmenting of the previously-dominant American-Western template. Whereas CNN provided the only established globally-available satellite television news operation at the time, 2003 audiences comprised of very different cultures (in the West as well as in the Arab world) and watched Al-Jazeera, Abu-Dhabi, or any one of a number of relatively new Arab-based satellite channels. Their journalists possessed different histories and different motivations and so constructed different templates through which to frame the Iraq War. For example, the satellite channel Al-Arabia even presented the conflict as 'Gulf War III' by taking the eight-year Iran–Iraq conflict as the first Gulf War and 1991 as the second. Meanwhile, CNN (US domestic) and CNN International (CNNI) actually split their coverage for the entire war. US audiences received coverage more in keeping with America's military and political centrality to the war, while CNNI aimed to provide a more internationalist perspective for viewers outside of the States.

However, given that the nationality of the embeds tended to reflect the composition of the 'coalition' forces, even the splintering broadcast market of 2003 did not significantly moderate the principally American discourse from the field. Indeed, 'new propaganda' involves twenty-first-century warfare fought through the niche biases of proliferating news networks, catering to increasingly geographically, culturally and politically fragmented television audiences. Fox TV is the obvious example. However, even CNN's split-coverage provided one relatively isolationist vision of the war for US audiences and another for Europe and the Rest of the World. Audiences are increasingly able to consume a version of news that does not challenge their (or their nation's) cultural and political outlook, or, conversely, choose one that does. And, given that Fox News was the ratings-winner amongst cable networks in the States, it is clear that audiences are choosing the former over the latter. Mostly, though, the 'choices' in terms of US networks involved gradations of support for the war, from Fox TV through to public service broadcasters (e.g. C-SPAN). However, had the Arab networks launched English-language or subtitled versions of their TV output (as well as on the internet), then the mostly pro-war breaking news would have been more effectively challenged in the West.

The new global spaces covered by the Arab media, however, did pose some difficulties for American news management. One of the key issues for television broadcasters in 2003 (as considered in Chapter 2) was whether or not to run footage of the several American POWs paraded on Iraqi TV on 23 March and rebroadcast on the globally-available Al-Jazeera. CBS was the only major US network to show the footage, although later (apparently after contact from the Pentagon) it ran it with the POWs' faces blurred. CNN meanwhile did not broadcast the video but repeatedly showed a still taken from Al-Jazeera that did not identify features but nonetheless depicted uniformed corpses on the floor. In effect, the fact that Al-Jazeera made these images available to a global audience provided an excuse for Western broadcasters (particularly in the UK – see also p.xx, above) to use them. Firstly, they were able to cite that these were 'already in the public domain', and secondly, Al-Jazeera broadcasting this footage became as significant a part of the news story as the actual capture of the POWs.

Concerns were expressed in the USA over families learning of the death or capture of their loved ones from TV. And the mother of Joseph Hudson did indeed recognize one of the POWs as her son whilst watching a subscription Filipino channel in Almagordo, El Paso. This is a prime example of the increasing 'leakage' of news in globally and reflexively attentive markets of the twenty-first century, in which anything and everything is potentially available – and magnified – in the 'global village' that even McLuhan could not have envisaged. However, the increasing spill-over of niche news programming in the global arena, evident in the heightened reflexive media environment of the Iraq War, shapes public opinion near and far. Jonathan Raban (2003: 6), for example, observes,

> Once, jingoistic news broadcasts were received only by the domestic audiences whose morale they were designed to boost. Now when

> Walter Rodgers [CNN embed] growls into the mike that he and his boys are going to 'bite a chunk off Baghdad', he can be heard and seen by Islamists around the world as the living embodiment of America in her war of conquest and revenge.

Raban compares the Reuters footage[27] depicting Palestinians celebrating the attacks of September 11, 2001 with some of the images from US cable coverage of the Iraq War, and argues that the revulsion felt by Americans at these scenes should at least inform a recognition of Arab responses to the triumphalism of some of the US embeds (ibid.). For the US cable channels, however, is it is precisely the gung-ho televisuality – the flag-waving banners, drum-beating soundtrack and patriotic language – that deliver audience-share. With the exception of the public service broadcasters, news networks simply cannot afford to be labelled as 'unpatriotic' or not to reflect the national mood, particularly during the times of war and catastrophe that seem increasingly to define news and politics in the USA in the new millennium.

It is unsurprising then that whilst most of the US networks refused to broadcast the Iraqi TV images, they instead went into an overdrive of revulsion. An MSNBC news anchor, for example, talked with David Kay, a former chief nuclear weapons inspector in Iraq and 'NBC analyst':

> **Kay:** The problem is I did look at that tape a second time and it's a tape I hope most of the American people do not see. Not because I think they shouldn't see it to understand the nature of the regime because I'm afraid it would be far too upsetting for the families of those. It's one of the most disturbing images I've ever seen.
>
> **Anchor:** And I would have to agree and as I said earlier I'd be lying if I said I wasn't still shaken by the image and I don't even want to go into describing what we saw. (*MSNBC, live, 23 March 2003*)

The tone and content of these remarks were typical of US-based broadcasters, although in the UK, news responses were more measured, and most news programmes eventually showed extracts from the tape. On the same day, *Channel 4 News* did not show the video footage, but instead used five stills, each depicting one of the prisoners:

Jonathan Rugman (narrating over film report): Another Iraqi propaganda scoop, the first interviews with American POWs, which we're not showing because they breach the Geneva Convention. (*Channel 4 News, 23 March 2003*)

However, although the Geneva Convention was stated by a number of networks as a reason not to broadcast part or all of this footage, of course governments, not broadcasters, are signatories.[28] Eventually though, the dissemination of images of the POWs in the British print media and elsewhere reached a critical mass at which the running of the video was no longer newsworthy in itself, and became merely part of the documentation of the early days of the war.

The problem with the reflexive environment of real-time news of warfare is that once a story or even rumour is picked up and run with by one news organization, it becomes difficult for others not to follow. Indeed, there was intense pressure on networks just to get the news 'out there'. One CNN producer based in Britain, in an off-the-record seminar, acknowledged that a key quandary for the networks was, whether to run with a story without verification and risk having to later withdraw it, or hold back and watch a competitor break the news first. This is quite an extraordinary acknowledgement and demonstrates to what extent what was seen on television screens was paced by an information flow sourced by rumour and the fragments supplied by embeds. In short, the multiple embedded snapshots scattered any potential consistent or ordered news narrative on the Iraq War. More journalists, citing more sources, capturing more images, with more feeds to more networks, provided the fog that was the media war. Perhaps this is a fair reflection of the fragmented and scattered nature of warfare, but at least with coverage of the Gulf War, news networks conveyed a slower, clearer, and more considered narrative of warfare, although, ironically, from less information.

CRITICAL DISCOURSES

Phillip Knightley (2003: 9) compares the embedded journalists of World War I with those of the Iraq War: 'The modern embeds, too, soon lost all distinction between warrior and correspondent.' He claims to have found only one instance of an embed who 'wrote a story highly critical of the behaviour of US troops and which went against the official account of what had occurred' (ibid). The exception to which Knightley refers was not even a report from a TV correspondent but was filed by William Branigin of the *Washington Post*, entitled: 'A Gruesome Scene on Highway 9: 10 Dead After Vehicle Shelled at Checkpoint'. Branigan was embedded with the US Army's 3rd Infantry Division and he reports on US soldiers opening fire on a civilian van at a checkpoint on 31 March:

> 'Fire a warning shot,' [Capt. Ronny Johnson] ordered as the vehicle kept coming. Then, with increasing urgency, he told the platoon to shoot a 7.62mm machine-gun round into its radiator. 'Stop [messing] around!' Johnson yelled into the company radio network when he still saw no action being taken. Finally, he shouted at the top of his voice, 'Stop him, Red 1, stop him!'
>
> That order was immediately followed by the loud reports of 25mm cannon fire from one or more of the platoon's Bradleys. About half a dozen shots were heard in all.
>
> 'Cease fire!' Johnson yelled over the radio. Then, as he peered into his binoculars from the intersection on Highway 9, he roared at the platoon leader, 'You just [expletive] killed a family because you didn't fire a warning shot soon enough!'
>
> So it was that on a warm, hazy day in central Iraq, the fog of war descended on Bravo Company.

In Washington, the Pentagon issued a statement saying the vehicle was fired on after the driver ignored shouted orders and warning shots. The shooting, it said, was under investigation. This example, as Knightley suggests, is an exception to the mostly consensual discourse produced by embedded correspondents. However, there were two other key groups of journalists covering the war outside of the embed system. Firstly, the hundreds of reporters gathered at the million-dollar 'CentCom' media centre built at Dohar, Qatar, where the US military were to provide official daily briefings on the progress of the war and, secondly, those in the war zone but not embedded, a group that became known as the 'unilaterals'.

The journalists gathered at CentCom soon realized that they were to become at best peripheral to the reporting of the war. The wooden easels and charts of 1991 had been replaced with huge plasma screens providing a cinematic view for the benefit of primarily American audiences.

Moreover, unlike the Gulf War, the embeds provided the substantive material to satisfy continuous broadcast news programming and millions of column inches around the world. Given the flow of instantaneous images from all over Iraq (which, after all, was where the story was) it quickly became apparent that Centcom was a mere sideshow in the media war. Whereas in 1991 Pentagon briefings actually provided the newsworthy images and genuinely new information which served to anchor and narrate hours of pool footage, Centcom briefings were often shown in a smaller window on TV screens in 2003, in the shadow of live images beamed from Iraq. The media currency of the military briefing was effectively devalued in 2003, and the whole Dohar set-up was a coup of news management, of new propaganda.

Michael Wolff, a writer for *New York* magazine, argues that the CentCom operation was 'bogus' in terms of the restricted and sanitized view it delivered of the war:

> Everybody here was having the same perfectly Groundhog Day experience: you woke up only to repeat the day before, and, no matter what you did or said or thought, you were helpless to effect a change in the next day. So every day everybody asked the same questions about Basra and the supply lines and the whereabouts of the WMDs and Saddam, and got the same answers. (*2003: 6*)

Eventually, Wolff asked at a briefing, 'Why are we here? Why should we stay? What's the value of what we're learning at this million dollar press centre'? (ibid.) He claims that this question (which received applause from his press colleagues) led to his marginalization and persecution by the US media managers, including the arrival of 3,000 hate emails. Wolff's account demonstrates that the unprecedented management of the media in twenty-first-century warfare has certain costs for journalists who are prepared to publicly challenge the message and the conditions imposed for delivering that message.

The greater the independence of the journalist, it seems, the potentially greater the personal cost. For example, the unilateral British ITN journalist Terry Lloyd was shot dead in his car by US marines (mistaking it for an Iraqi vehicle) and two of his accompanying cameramen were reported as 'missing'. On 8 April 2003, three cameramen were killed by Americans: Tareq Ayoub died following a single US missile hitting the al-Jazeera's

Baghdad office, and Taras Protsyuk (Reuters) and Jose Couso (Spain's Telecino channel) both died as a result of an American tank shelling the Palestine Hotel. The hotel in question was actually the base for many of the journalists covering the war in Baghdad. For this reason, there were numerous witnesses to the shelling of the 15th floor, including evidence from footage shot by France 3 Television, which contributed to the exposure of considerable contradictions in US accounts of this incident.

The question over the US deliberate targeting of journalists has also arisen in the greater anxieties and insecurities of the post-September 11, 2001 environment (see Marie Gillespie (2002) and www.afterseptember11.tv). For example, the BBC's Nik Gowing undertook an investigation into the November 2001 US bombing of the Al-Jazeera office in Qatar, from where video of Osama bin Laden had been broadcast during the war over Afghanistan. He concluded that, 'the US military makes no effort to distinguish between legitimate satellite uplinks for broadcast news communications and the identifiable radio or satellite communications belonging to "the enemy"' (8 April 2002).[29] So, in February 2003, al-Jazeera TV, determined to avoid being targeted by the US military again, provided the Pentagon with the actual coordinates of the network's Baghdad office.[30] Clearly this did not prevent the network from being hit again, and in such circumstances it appears that media organizations and their personnel can do little to protect themselves if reporting from outside of the systems laid down by the Pentagon.

The extent to which the targeting of independent journalists is deliberate and part of Pentagon policy will be written into the history of the Iraq War. Knightley (2003: 11), for example, is convinced that the Pentagon will not accept more reporting from the side of the enemy, and 'the occasional shots fired at "media sites" are not accidental and that war correspondents may now be targets'. Robert Fisk, the British *Independent* journalist, goes further in articles entitled 'Is There Some Element in the US Military that Wants to Take Out Journalists'? (9 April 2003) and 'Did the US Murder These Journalists'? (26 April 2003). In the latter, he points out that American journalists are not even investigating these incidents, but warns them that, 'They should – because they will be next' (p. 17). And it is the impartiality of many journalists (although particularly American), which has been compromised through their relations with the military, that has appeared more defining of the Iraq War than other recent conflicts. In this respect,

Fisk provides a stark contrast, in providing the most effective critical commentary on the war and the information war in the UK broadsheet media.

In all accounts, what is clear is that journalists, their safety, actions and sources, are all increasingly entrenched as subjects of war reporting itself. The new propaganda of the 'up close and personal' mass embedding of correspondents dominated news output and obscured critical discourse on the war. With many journalists already in Baghdad before the American troops, some networks ran with the story of the safety of their personnel in respect of a need for the marines to arrive quickly to fill the dangerous vacuum created by the melting away of the regime. David Chater, for example, reported live for Sky News from the streets just outside the Palestine Hotel, Baghdad. Complete with flak jacket and helmet and PRESS emblazoned across his front and back, he scans the horizon nervously and contemplates the failure of any marines to reach his position as yet:

> Those tanks, those marines are still not with us. They still haven't arrived as far as we're concerned. There is no sense of freedom here, in fact quite the opposite. The front line is squeezing in around us and so is the sense of danger. We don't know what's taking the marines so long. If they're not facing any resistance why don't they keep pushing on up this road to the Press Centre here? But it's getting pretty dangerous for the remaining press here at the moment because there are armed men around, there are people taking cameras off us, there are people shooting and beating people up just a block away from here while the marines are six blocks down that way so we're waiting their arrival pretty anxiously. (*Sky News, live, 9 April 2003*)

News of some 'resistance' nearby from off-camera causes Chater to end his report abruptly and walk out of the shot.

Less than two hours later, Sky News returns to live coverage of the area outside the hotel as US marines in tanks and other military vehicles finally arrive. Chater is visibly relieved and (minus helmet) begins strolling around the marines (who have taken up various positions on the ground) being followed by his cameraman. He greets individual troops and informs them they are going out live and prompts them to identify themselves to the watching global audience:

Chater: Hi you're live on Sky News right now. How's it been coming in?

Marine: Er it's been pretty good coming in here as a matter of fact. Is this it?

Chater: (smiling) Yeah this is just about it you've got nothing else really to take.

Marine: Well let's hope so! And I hope they won't be hiding and a-shooting at us that's the only thing I'm worried about.

Chater: Has there been a lot of resistance a lot of sniper fire?

Marine: A lot of sniper fire, RPGs, but all they do is shoot at us and drop their weapons and then run and take off their uniforms and then they go back to their lives, so.

Chater: I've been seeing them doing it too, so be careful. What's your name? You're going out to America now as well.

Marine: My name's Timothy [inaudible] United States Marine Corps.

Chater: Bloody good to see you.

Marine: Thanks a lot.

Chater: Thank you. Be careful. (*Sky News, live, 9 April 2003*)

Chater's relief at feeling secure again surrounded by US marines is palpable; however, his identification with the troops adds a partial and even cheerleading tone to his reporting. The extract also illustrates the irony arising from the relatively well-informed journalists in their globally-connected hotel compared with the isolated marines arriving in separate divisions into Baghdad. The marine asks Chater if they had reached their objective, 'Is this it'?

The ability of correspondents to interview soldiers live on air whilst in the midst of operations was one of the defining features of the TV coverage in 2003. David Bowden, for example, another reporter for Sky, spent several hours crouched down in the sand with marines who had come across a number of the enemy in the port of Umm Qasr on 23 March. Every so often he would interrupt one of the commanding officers for an 'update' for the watching global audience. This type of reporting affords an incredibly close and personal view of warfare. Yet it is a closeness and detail of mere fragments of the war in very specific times and contexts. The minutiae of warfare in the shape of personal experiences of correspondents and soldiers served to compress media coverage into a series of disconnected snapshots. This may provide compelling television for some but it provides little opportunity for sustained critical media or public discourse to emerge on the overall waging of the war and its longer-term consequences.

OVEREXPOSURE

With expensive and mass deployment by many news organizations, media events (which warfare has become) have a very limited shelf-life as resources cannot be sustained indefinitely. Post-war coverage is inevitably considerably reduced, ironically, even if the consequences of the fighting of war are greater. News times matter, as it is during the most intensive and extensive coverage that public perceptions of warfare are principally forged. Moreover, instant-access journalism afforded a new perception of fighting war that conveniently fitted the genre of reality TV in demand amongst Western audiences. Armando Iannucci (2003: 16) for example, observes: 'Programmed over the past few years to watch endless numbing footage of ordinary people trapped by television producers in an artificial situation, we, the viewers, felt we were watching reality TV on a massive scale.' However, the fundamentals of the reality TV format involve intensive exposure of the minutiae of minute-by-minute existence of those participating. Beyond real-time coverage of the *Big Brother* house, there is little left for audiences. And very few of the instant-celebrities created from immediate and extensive exposure actually endure in public consciousness until the next series and the next set of house-mates. We can speculate that the similar nature of the coverage of the Iraq War (particularly on Fox and Sky News) will produce equally ephemeral impressions and memories. Jean Baudrillard (1994: 63) argues that a certain amnesia resides in the media event: 'Overexposed to the media, underexposed to memory. Built-in obsolescence, as with any consumer article . . . Forgetting is built into the event itself in the profusion of information and details, just as obsolescence is built into the object in the profusion of useless accessories.'

The Gulf War provides the most useful contrast in this respect, in terms of the very different modes of coverage then, and that the Iraq War is in a number of ways the product of the media's gradual unpicking of the closure of the 1991 war. For instance, despite the involving experience for audiences watching on television at the time, and the occasional dramatic (or rather, dramatized) scene, most of what was shown and seen was actually peripheral to the war itself. In 1991 the world witnessed only war at the margins as this was precisely the space that journalists inhabited for most of the time. It is unsurprising, then, that the televising of the Gulf War sits awkwardly in social memory. In addition to the 'derealizing' tendencies (which I consider in Chapter 4), the emphasis on the moment and on heightened expectations of what potentially might be witnessed by audiences contributed to 'a war that produced no memory' (Cumings, 1992: 103). Moreover, this is how the restricted picture of the Gulf War afforded by television news then appears today, in the shadow of the acclaimed unprecedented access of reporters in showing the actuality of the war of 2003.

However, the actuality of the Iraq War involved the prioritizing of image-dissemination over news-gathering and time over content. Effective analysis and understanding were substituted with the self-evidency of immediate images as the threshold for what was included as news was lowered. Commentator prompts reveal the utter emptiness of much of the live coverage, with 'let's listen in' or 'let's watch and see what's going down' directing audiences to adopt reality TV modes of consumption.

The immediacy of the mostly constructed news talk of 1991 was replaced in 2003 with an obviousness of the live image. The apparent omnipresence mediated by the embeds and the fixed cameras delivering 24-hour views of Baghdad served, however, to lull audiences into conflating spectacle with reality. New propaganda essentially involves selling this illusion, which is what the embed system and principally the saturation of live TV images delivered for the Bush administration. What is significant, therefore, is what the real-time mass dissemination of images obliterated from view and from memory. And it is this, the unseen of the Gulf Wars, to which I now turn.

Chapter 4

Bodies fallen in time – the bloody resonance of battle

> On the screen, the B52s took off for the nth raid against Baghdad or Basra. It was difficult to know the number of casualties these cities had suffered, for neither the Americans nor Saddam Hussein had an interest in admitting them. But the deafness being induced began with the fact that no reference was made to what was already known. Four or five times a day the public received a TV lesson about how to become deaf to the voice of their memory, of their conscience or of their imagination.
>
> (*John Berger, 'In the land of the deaf'*, Guardian, *2 March 1991*)

Writing at the end of the Gulf War, the cultural critic Berger implicates a collusion of censorship between Coalition governments, their media, the Iraqi dictatorship, and Western television audiences. For the most part this was a self-serving self-censorship founded upon selling and per-petuating the myth that 'sanitized coverage' equates to 'clean warfare'. The networks absorbed Pentagon briefings and their message of 'pin-point accuracy' into their daily schedules. If nothing else it helped fill endless coverage in the absence of actuality footage.

The precision warfare myth of the Gulf War, however, has endured in Western consciousness almost to the same extent as the memory of the bloodiness of Vietnam it was declared to obscure. The CNN view of the Gulf War effectively stymied anti-war sentiment in the USA and Fox News' coverage of the Iraq War provided a publicly-mediated space for the cheerleaders of war to find new levels of legitimacy, and for the rest at least to find reassurance in patriotism packaged by the hour. A con-sequence of the increased 'choice' brought via the proliferation of news channels between the Gulf Wars is that audiences can more easily tune in to a niche version of warfare that does not so easily disturb, and opt out from a global consciousness and memory of suffering. In a multi-channelled world, the remote control has become a most effective sanitizing instrument.

In this way, there is a decreasing need for governments, military, media and audiences to collude in censorship. Moreover, it remains the case that graphic images of war involving the investment of Western lives often do not emerge until some time after the end of the cessation of conflict, if at all. In such later times these images are often more palatable to Western audiences, particularly when the event being depicted has receded further into history. Once outside of the event time phase of war (identified in Chapter 3) images cannot feed in to reflexively affect the event being covered as news, i.e. when the outcome of events has already been determined.

The impact of graphic images of the injured and the dead then is said to diminish with the 'body lag',[31] which Kahn defines as 'The time between the moment a body drops or is mangled in war and is photographed and the moment that class of photographs reaches dissemination on a social scale' (1992: 43). In this chapter, I explore the ways in which images of suffering and dead bodies are translated into new memory, including those images previously unseen, or not widely disseminated, until some time after the event which they depict has ended. Those images mediated in later times appear to warrant less justification in their publication and attract less public and political attention. However, as *new* images, to what extent do they retain the capacity to shock and to reshape memories of the event from which they were taken?

The historicization of graphic bodily *news* images through their repetition (in books, movies, museums, etc.) affords them an acceptability rarely acquired nearer to the time of their capture and when displayed in fewer modes of representation. So, there are two key processes that influence responses to graphic images of Western bodies and injury in our media: firstly, their presentation as distant past, as 'history'; and secondly, through their repetition and thus recognition, through which they may become easier to 'read'. One of the key examples of a shift from minimal to mass exposure of a now iconic image of a body from the Gulf War is a photograph taken by Ken Jarecke entitled 'Iraqi Soldier'.

ANONYMOUS CORPSE – THE JARECKE IMAGE

At the end of the Iraq War, a column of Iraqi forces were caught retreating northwards by Coalition air forces on the Basra Road, since known as the 'Highway of Death'. This seems an appropriate label given that the Iraqis could not escape or hide and so provided easy targets for the forces in the skies above them. Jarecke's photograph, taken on the 28 February 1991, shows a charred Iraqi soldier still upright at the windscreen of a burnt-out vehicle. *Life Magazine*, based in the USA, first agreed to publish this image and had the photo laid out in a double page spread, approved by the magazine's picture editor and overall editor. However, the photo was pulled at the last minute by the highest level of management of this publication. Jarecke was not successful elsewhere in the United States at this time, with the leading picture agency Associated Press refusing to distribute it because it was 'a little too graphically, gruesomely violent'.[32] However, the *Observer*, a Sunday newspaper in the UK, printed the photo in black-and-white deep inside the newspaper on page 9 on 3 March. This was reprinted the following day in the *Observer's* sister-daily, the *Guardian*, with the merits of its publication being defended by its picture editor, Eamonn McCabe, in an accompanying article entitled 'Dilemma of the Grisly and the Gratuitous'. McCabe asks, 'why should we wait for the history books to be published before being faced with the gruesome reality of death in conflict? As many as 100,000 Iraqi soldiers may have been killed in the Gulf war, so why have so few dead bodies been shown in the British press?' He suggests that the answer partly lies in fear of upsetting readers. In fact, the *Observer* soon received several hundred letters from readers questioning the need for this 'real' image of war to be printed, and not least because it jarred with the context of the widely-expressed relief and euphoria of 'victory' over Saddam in and through the Western media at this time.

Although the photograph is seen as a visual medium of 'high definition' (McLuhan, 1964: 22), the black-and-white reproduction on newsprint inevitably degrades the quality and definition of an image. The Jarecke image would have had much wider impact if it had been reproduced in colour, and the *Observer* would no doubt have attracted even greater criticism for using it gratuitously. However, even in its black-and-white form, the charred mould of the face, including the detail of the remains of the teeth and the upright position of the corpse, contribute to a shocking picture. But, it is the context of the almost total absence of similar images in the British press (and television) that ensured that the Jarecke photo ruptured readers' sanitized daily view of the war. Furthermore, at this time the body lag was simply too short for most newspaper editors/owners and broadcasters to risk alienating their readers and audiences.

However, the anonymity of the corpse – we know very little about its history other than it probably being an Iraqi – reduces the impact of the image. For audiences, a dispassionate response (or no response) is more likely if the life (and thus the death) of the corpse is more difficult to read, and not least if the body is 'other' in terms of culture, nation or religion. In the same way, the display of images of the dead (or of the imprisoned or tortured living) that imply the pain of others and whose life can be fully imagined can provoke greater outrage. The Coalition POWs paraded on Iraqi TV in both Gulf Wars and the US bodies shown during the Iraq War are a case in point, and not least because of their public and particularly voyeuristic display.

The blurring of the faces of the captured and dead US soldiers by some news networks in 2003 (who claimed this was to prevent possible identification by relatives viewing in the States) also functioned to reduce their recognition by wider US audiences and thus their impact. For as Sontag (2003: 70) argues, 'With our dead, there has always been a powerful interdiction against showing the naked face.' Anonymity in the representation of the body, in this way, also conveys greater respect. The carbonized face of the Iraqi soldier in the Jarecki photograph, despite some of the horrific detail of its features, partly *de*humanizes the body, and thus reduces rather than increases its impact. However, despite the reluctance by much of the Western news media to use Jarecke's photograph at the time of the Gulf War, it has since achieved wide publication, and not least as a template on coverage of the Iraq War. And it is to the post-1991 dissemination of this image as the subject of an extended body lag that I now turn.

*   *   *

Despite the very cautious first print publication of Jarecke's photograph, it did appear on a Western front page, although not until almost seven years after the end of the Gulf War. Early in 1998 the crisis over UNSCOM weapons inspectors being denied access to Saddam's presidential palaces brought the Coalition, or at least the USA and the UK, very close to the use of military force (so-called 'Desert Thunder') against Iraq. The front page of the *New Statesman* of 20 February carried an almost full-page version of this photograph, significantly larger and more prominent than the *Guardian* and *Observer* prints of 1991. Moreover, the image was reproduced in full colour.

By this time, however, the extended body lag enabled the image to be viewed as a historical document, rather than as a news photograph, being employed as a visual template on the 1998 crisis by the *New Statesman*. One can equate the passage of time with a less derealized view of the war, providing a new context within which previously unacceptable images become tolerable. In this same time-frame the distance between the viewer/reader and the 'reality' of the event can be seen to contract. What is striking is that the full-colour gloss and high definition of the *New Statesman* reproduction is so at odds with the dominant representation of the war in 1991, particularly given that this image was available at the time. However, is this template more than just a historical reminder, and does it reconfigure the dominant visual memory of the Gulf War from that originally seen in print and on television at the time?

New memory involves a mediated re-negotiation of past events, although, as Sontag (2003: 85) argues, our sense of a distant past can be revised and constructed through the dissemination of new or unseen images

> with the posthumous shocks engineered by the circulation of hitherto unknown photographs. Photographs that everyone recognizes are now a constituent part of what a society chooses to think about, or declares that it has chosen to think about. It calls these ideas 'memories', and that is, over the long run, a fiction.

Sontag's crucial point here is that we should not confuse the recognizable mediated image with collective memory, for the latter she sees as the directing of narratives about what is important to a society at a given time, as opposed to a shared remembering. This perspective implicates the artificial and external nature of that which is often called collective memory, for it is found in the archive, the media, and is shaped by ideologies. If an image is held up often enough in these ways as representative of an event, person or place, then inevitably there will occur a degree of collective recognition. And even though individual memories may contain quite different and changing perceptions of the same image, some images maintain continuity over time through their external, mediated representations and the context in which they are placed in those representations. Whether this continuity (and discontinuity) constitutes collective memory (and collective amnesia) depends upon the influence one affords to external sources over the human mind. This is really the challenge in conceptualizing new memory.

However, in terms of the censorship or restriction in representing graphic images of warfare, the very debates over the merits or otherwise of their publication or screening can shape their historical significance. Thus, as with debates over censorship in popular culture, curiosity is aroused in the unseeing or unhearing audience, particularly when broadcasters impose their own ban (e.g. over explicit song lyrics or video images). Public controversy over the representation of a shocking image simply adds to its history. The more narratives there are threaded around the existence of an image, the more it is likely to be seen and reproduced, and the more likely it is to endure in social memory. In this way, the Jarecke image is essentially a *contested* representation of the Gulf War given its relatively restricted circulation and dissemination at the time, and, moreover, the disjuncture it represents in relation to the sanitized and dominant media imaging of the war.

Despite the debates that undoubtedly add to the photograph's historical significance, it has become iconic of the other horrors of the road to Basra that were filmed but never broadcast. That is to say, its familiarity as *the* shocking image of the Gulf War has displaced others that exist but even today have yet to be published or broadcast. Robert Fisk (2003: 21), for example, observes that ITV were filming the horrors of the Basra Road 'for the record' (according to one of their cameramen) which cannot be shown, 'First because it is not "appropriate" to depict such reality on breakfast-time TV. Second because, if what we saw was shown on television, no one would ever again agree to support a war.' The photograph of the dead Iraqi soldier in this way acts as a *sign* of other casualties of the war, those documented and those that went unwitnessed.

However, unlike the multiple and extensive signs of the previous war fought by the USA in a mediated age, the bloody consequences of the Gulf War were tangential to the Western view. And the historical record does not seem to have been effective in retrospectively challenging this perspective, as John Taylor (1998: 183) argues, 'Terrible images and accounts belong to the war's peripheral history.'[33] One reason for this, as I have suggested, is that the initial televising of the war was so marginal to its fundamental realities that the news channels that delivered this sanitized but compelling footage have reinforced the event as first seen, through templates and in forging their own histories. CNN has been the principal arbiter of this televisual memory.

Because of the initial lack of popular support in the UK, the onset of the Iraq War brought with it a whole new set of anti-war discourses which needed a visual slogan around which to gather support. That is to say that what was initially billed as 'Gulf War II' inevitably drew parallels through templates originating from 1991 news programmes, as I have shown. In the UK at least, it was the Jarecke photograph that fulfilled this need as the very antithesis of the ready visual associations of the Gulf War (as outlined in Chapter 2). This photograph was even used on an A5-sized flyer that I found stuck to a university wall advertising a local anti-war meeting in February 2003. The image of the Iraqi soldier had been used as part of the frame of the flyer, superimposed over Bush and Blair, grinning and shaking hands, with 'STOP THE WAR!' printed above their heads. Its poor reproduction, photocopied in black-and-white, left the soldier looking a less human and ghostly greyish-white. The combination of images is obviously intended to directly connect the political decision-makers with the brutal outcomes of warfare. The flyer is also an example of the remediation of the Jarecke photograph outside of the mainstream media and illustrates how even originally censored and/or shocking images can be publicly disseminated in other ways.

In the build-up to the Iraq War, this photograph was published more widely in the British press than at any other time previously. For example, it was reproduced in black-and-white, to accompany Fisk's article mentioned above (*Independent on Sunday*, 26 January 2003).

The wider dissemination of the Jarecke photo (at least in the UK) acts to compete with the living memory of the first mediated representations of the Gulf War. And an essential problematic of new memory is in distinguishing between a mediated re-negotiation of the past in changing and new representations, and the complexities of the impact of these changes in shaping individual and collective perceptions of events. This is especially so when the previously unseen image or unheard account over a period of time is repeated to the extent that it becomes iconic.

The *Guardian* of 14 February 2003 devoted its *G2* section entirely to 'The Unseen Gulf War', which I considered in Chapter 2. Several of the photographs in this publication depicted dismembered and carbonized bodies and the body parts of Iraqi soldiers. A number of these pictures were taken on the Basra Road, north of Kuwait City, as the Coalition literally 'cleared up' the Iraqi dead. These close-up, shocking images contrast starkly with much of the television documentary footage of the Basra Road shot after the destruction of the retreating Iraqi forces. Often documentaries screened in the UK have obscured the graphic detail of the Iraqi dead, either through the use of film taken from the air, or (and especially soon after the war) by using footage shot after the clearing-up operation had been completed, when all that remained were the burnt and wrecked vehicles of the convoy with all signs of their occupants removed.

Jarecke's Iraqi soldier photograph is included in 'The Unseen Gulf War', this time in colour and spread across the two centre pages of the newspaper section, along with a poem that originally accompanied its publication in 1991. In the pre-Iraq War context, these graphic images of the Gulf War would not be seen as unpatriotic. In this way they could at best function as a pre-emptive template to the anticipated sanitized coverage, for readers would be less likely to find their publication acceptable during time of war itself. In other words, images of this nature would be perceived as unpatriotic by audiences who tend to be supportive of national military forces when in action even if they are unconvinced of the justification for that action. The best that certain sections of the print media could hope for was to produce definitively different images to the reality-obscuring though visually dramatic fireworks that we were told were 'precision' strikes during the Gulf War.

COVERING THE BODY

In Chapter 2 I explored how new memory of the Vietnam War has shaped military–media relations since and set the parameters for US mainstream media reporting of the Gulf War. There was a certain degree of approval in the US administration and military of the initial

TV images of the war, not least given the extent to which airtime was filled with pool or 'pre-censored' footage (even Defence Secretary Dick Cheney complimented CNN on their battle damage assessments at the opening of the war). Western audiences were confronted with few disturbing pictures of the consequences of warfare. Those images that did provoke outrage tended to be own-goals on the part of Iraqi propaganda disseminated via state TV and then remediated globally: the parading of the so-called 'human shields' in August 1990 (as I show in Chapter 5) and in January 1991 the visibly bruised and shaken captured Coalition pilots (as I showed in Chapter 2).

The continuity of the American-inspired discourse of 'smart' and 'precision' bombing was (albeit briefly) shattered on 13 February with their bombing of a 'bunker' at Amiriya, Baghdad. This incident was perhaps the most highly contested and scrutinized of the war, and in particular on the television stations which carried the most graphic images of the Iraqi wounded and dead.

Around 400 Iraqi civilians, mostly women and children, were killed in a direct hit by the Coalition. The USA claimed that this building was an Iraqi command and control installation into which civilians had been moved shortly before it was hit. One of their explanations for this attack was that the bunker was pre-programmed into a database of targets but the latest intelligence available (or at least to the extent of information being entered into the database) did not reveal the presence of civilians at this location. The Iraqi Government meanwhile maintained that the bunker was an air raid shelter.

To a Western television audience who had been for some time anaesthetized by a succession of derealized images, the sight of charred bodies being carried out of the smouldering bunker in Baghdad was, at the very least, a break in the perceptual continuity of the coverage. There was little in the way of a body lag in the breaking of this story as the world's media were quickly escorted to the scene by their Iraqi minders. The available images posed the first major challenge for broadcasters and other media of the war as to what to show and how to report what appeared to be a terrible loss of civilian lives. Some of the journalists taken to the scene and a nearby hospital the morning following the air raid were careful to differentiate the incident and the Iraqi response to it from what they had previously been shown by the Iraqis. For example, the BBC's Jeremy Bowen, reporting for NBC's *Nightly News – America at War*, made precisely this point: 'There were dreadful scenes outside the hospital. None of this was set up for our cameras. It was real grief and real anger' (13 February 1991).

The pictures of bodies, and survivors suffering burn wounds, were the first images of the war to re-connect graphically the notion of bombing with bodily violence, a connection previously obscured through effective media management and Coalition censoring. In response, the USA put all their efforts into attempting to legitimize the target, by spinning a discourse of precision warfare. In this, to an extent, they were aided by a news media providing full coverage of military briefings obsessed with the logistics of the campaign and not its consequences. The official discourse in accounting for the deaths at Amiriya thus shifted to representations of the bombs and the bunker themselves.

At the Pentagon briefing of February 14 the commonplace maps and charts were produced, this time identifying the location and function of the bunker. NBC used the bold text, 'COMMAND AND CONTROL FACILITY' to label the building in a full colour video graphic, effectively closing down alternative explanations.

Further NBC graphics depicted the close proximity of the 'command and control facility' to a school and a mosque, effectively legitimizing the target as 'non-civilian' through it being surrounded by 'civilian' sites which were not targeted or hit. NBC overlaid a central strap line 'THE BUNKER' across the screen, unambiguously reinforcing the explanation detailed in the briefing. Furthermore, NBC adopted the military cartography and employed vivid colour graphics to represent the actual bombing run of the night before, drawing attention to the apparent ease with which the '15ft STEEL REINFORCED CONCRETE' was penetrated by the US attack.

It is precisely the form of this representation of the war, the 'informational event', that, Jean Baudrillard argues, substitutes for the real: 'It is a masquerade of information: branded faces delivered over to the prostitution of the image, the image of an unintelligible distress. No images of the field of battle, but images of masks, of blind or defeated faces, images of falsification' (1995 [1991]: 40).

According to Baudrillard, the use of a selection of images to portray or mediate real events leads to the 'contamination' of the real by 'the structural reality of images' (ibid. 46–7). This results in a virtual media event, which is open to speculation, interpretation and analysis ad infinitum. Indeed, with the bombing at Amiriya, the *showing* of the footage of the dead and injured entered reflexively into the news story itself. The 'layering' of competing discourses surrounding an event can function to obscure the 'facts' and significance of that event. In this case, the deaths of hundreds of innocent civilians and the undermining of the previously dominant language of precision warfare were overwhelmed by a profusion of analysis and counter-analysis. Television coverage was not only the principal source of this analysis but also provided the subject for it.

Dick Cheney, for example, speaking on the day following the bunker bombing, engaged in this very tactic of obfuscation, 'Some have suggested this morning on television, some of the "talking heads", that we've all grown familiar with in recent weeks as we've watched this affair unfold, that Saddam might deliberately be resorting to a practice of deliberately placing civilians in harm's way' (NBC, 14 February 1991). The Defence Secretary is not stating categorically that this is Iraqi policy, but appears confident in presenting it as a plausible explanation in connection with having heard it on TV, i.e. rather than from his own department's intelligence sources. This is emphasized in his repetition of the word 'deliberately' in the same sentence, above. Cheney's comments also reveal just how integrated the constant television presence had become in America's experience of and support for the war. Had US and other Western audiences viewed footage of the full horrors at Amiriya, this event might have irrevocably altered perceptions as to the declared 'smart' capabilities of military technology at this time. However, there were two fundamental reasons why this did not happen: firstly, US and UK broadcasters were not prepared to transmit such graphic images for fear of breaching guidelines and offending audiences, and secondly, the latter would rather not be faced with pictures that cause such distress.

Obviously there is great public pressure not to broadcast or publish images of warfare that are deemed unpatriotic or that at least are perceived to undermine the rhetoric that accompanies the placing of a country's forces in 'harm's way'. The censoring of the images of Amiriya is an example of this and as John Taylor (1998: 172) argues, the general tone of reporting during the Gulf War represents a 'movement in the press away from disconcerting knowledge towards comforting knowledge, away from harsh realities towards a squeamish denial of reality'. The 'harsh realities' of Amiriya, however, were recorded on film. And

Jordanian TV (JTV), for example, did air more graphic footage than that broadcast in the West, obtained from unedited CNN feeds and from Baghdad's World Television News (WTN). However, JTV withheld what they considered to be the most obscene images. Laurie Garrett, a writer for *Newsday*, viewed the unedited JTV footage in its entirety:

> Nearly all the bodies were charred into blackness; in some cases the heat had been so great that entire limbs were burned off. Among the corpses were those of at least six babies and ten children, most of them so severely burned that their gender could not be determined. Rescue workers collapsed in grief, dropping corpses; some rescuers vomited from the stench of the still-smouldering bodies. (1991: 32)

There was scant mention of the presence of any babies amongst the dead at Amiriya on US television. The pictures of bodies shown on most US networks did not convey the horror evident in Garrett's description. Most of the bodies shown being carried from the bunker were covered so that the full extent of their injuries was not visible. For example, the CBS *Evening News* of 13 February repeated footage of a body being carried out on a stretcher away from the bunker three times in a one-hour programme, including framing this image in its opening title sequence. Although CBS did air more graphic views of the effects of the bombing of the bunker, it selected a relatively sanitized view to anchor much of its coverage of this story. However, it was through the construction of the 'informational event' (Baudrillard, *op. cit.*: 40), as much as the selective use of visual images, that television news coverage of Amiriya was effectively sanitized. And it is to these issues of the language of censorship that I now turn.

THE SEEN UNSEEN

Part of what might be called the 'structure' of war, beyond the physical engagement of combat itself, is the rationalizing of the destruction of human life, the discursive legitimizing of engaging in armed conflict – a consciousness of warfare – that extends either side of the declaration of its beginning and its end. Television functions paradoxically in this respect, for it possesses the potential, and indeed the promise, to deliver very immediate, intense and unambiguous images of the consequences of war, but as a filter and through presenting an edited, partial and sanitized version of events, it also glorifies war. In this respect, in recent history, the medium has increasingly contributed to that which Elaine Scarry identifies as the 'structure of physical and perceptual events', notably:

> it requires both the reciprocal infliction of massive injury and the eventual disowning of the injury so that its attributes can be attributed elsewhere, as they cannot if they are permitted to cling to the original site of the wound, the human body. (1985: 64)

The 'disowning' of injury, or the way that it disappears from view, according to Scarry, is achieved in two ways: firstly, and simply, by means of 'omission' and secondly, by way of an 'active redescription of the event: the act of injuring, or the tissue that is to be injured, or the weapon that is to accomplish the injury is renamed' (1985: 66). The televising of the Gulf War enabled a fundamental disowning of injury at the time and, as I have already argued, a crystallizing of memory around a belief in precision strikes and 'limited' warfare. The totality of the coverage simply did not evoke images of 'the original site of the wound, the human body', to cite Scarry. During 1991 a number of euphemisms for death emerged in an 'acceptable' mediated language of war that has since become familiar to Western audiences through coverage of the War over Kosovo, Afghanistan, and the Iraq War. For example, the killing of innocent civilians is subsumed in the logistical expression 'collateral damage' and the accidental killing of one's own men and women is routinely and absurdly described as an act of 'friendly' fire.

The numerous US government and administration (re)descriptions of the Amiriya bunker, recycled in much of their media, effectively 'disowned the injury' that occurred there. Whereas the Iraqis maintained the bunker was an 'air raid shelter', the USA employed the logistical language of: 'command and control facility'; 'hardened bunker'; 'military target'; 'strategic site'; and 'military command center'. This discourse feeds the informational event of the Gulf War and is indicative of an increasingly sanitized view afforded to both the military and the media, as Shapiro (1997: 51) argues: 'The technologies that permitted killing in the absence of seeing had removed specific, suffering bodies similar to

the way they are effaced in the theoretical language of war, as war discourse has increasingly moved from images of flesh to images of weapons
and logistics.' The 'changing fields of perception' (Virilio, 1989: 7) of
news publics can be attributed most clearly to the transformations in
television and the changing expectations of what war looks like and how
it *should* 'look' to the military, broadcasters, and to audiences. In this
respect the paradox in television's mediation of war is evident: its relative 'success' is founded upon both its immediacy and the promise of
delivering the actuality of warfare, of scenes of combat and sites of war,
and yet, also, on the very non-fulfilment of this promise. For instance,
whenever television news in the West comes close to showing the real and
graphic human cost of war (and particularly that waged by its own
governments), it becomes a very reluctant messenger. CBS anchor Dan
Rather, before the airing of the bunker footage, for example, warns his
audience: 'Pictures of the Baghdad bombing include some graphic
scenes of the reality of war. We caution you that some may not be suit-
able for children' (CBS, 13 February 1991). Later, Rather suggests
(somewhat differently) that some viewers will not even want to be dis-
turbed by these images and thus should not watch: 'These images are
graphic – and some viewers, especially children, may not want to watch
our next report' (CBS, 14 February 1991). Furthermore, virtually all the
reports from Amiriya were pre-recorded and carefully edited, closing
down the immediacy of the bombing that would have been communicated with live on-location images. And few US broadcasters were prepared to risk showing more than a glimpse of the true carnage at
Amiriya for fear of offending audiences and becoming vulnerable to
being labelled 'unpatriotic', in the context of a war that was publicly perceived to be 'going well'.

Elsewhere in the US television schedules, the bombing of the
Amiriya bunker was the subject of analysis away from headline news
programming. The *MacNeill/Lehrer News Hour* on PBS, for example,
is a well-established series that makes a claim to 'news in depth' and
belongs to the 'public service' broadcasting genre in this respect, as
opposed to the ratings-chasing more commercially-oriented networks
such as CBS, ABC and CNN. Its hour-long programme of 14 February
1991 was mostly devoted to the bunker story. However, the footage
used from Amiriya was even more sanitized than the major networks'
coverage, with three stills used to illustrate a studio debate on the pos-

sible explanations for this tragedy. These depicted: a smouldering hole in the roof of the bunker; a distance shot of the same; and smoke rising from the entrance to the bunker alongside a fire-fighting vehicle. Perhaps these stills had been randomly pulled from the available footage, but they do not contain any view of the central subject of the story, namely civilian bodies. In effect they are images only of the absence of suffering and effectively disown injury, in Scarry's words, by means of 'omission'.

The programme's studio debate involved a six-way discussion between the following:

> Contributors in studio:
> Anchor
> James Schlesinger (former Secretary of Defence)
> Paul Nitze (former arms control negotiator)
> Leslie Gelb (*New York Times*)
> Rep. Craig Washington (Democrat, Texas)
> In Atlanta studio:
> Major Gen. Perry Smith (USAF, retired)

An extract taken from this half-hour discussion involving three of the contributors is reproduced in Figure 6. This illustrates the complexities of talk that reflects on the incident itself and an explanation of the same, and the media's treatment of both of these.

The television coverage of the Gulf War was seen to devalue the status of the 'expert', if simply because the extent of programming hours conveyed 'expertise' on the many. Baudrillard is one of the fiercest critics of the pre-eminence of this discourse in 1990–91 (as noted earlier in Chapter 2). Smith (in Figure 6) appears to reinforce Baudrillard's notion of an informational coating being layered on a particular event by way of speculation and interpretation ad nauseum. It is the *clarity* of the notion of an 'air raid shelter' as an explanation for the deaths of civilians that Smith appears to be objecting to, as much as to the idea in itself. His claim to offer 'at least six alternative' explanations relating to the bunker reveals the very obfuscating function of his contribution.

The journalist Gelb, meanwhile, is determined that the bombing at Amiriya will not shape the progression of the war ('It will not turn out to be a watershed') and concurs with Smith in challenging what he

Smith: I would suggest that the media has to be a little careful not to grab the story as it comes out of Saddam's propaganda factory, too quickly, until we can take a look at it and make sure we know what's going on.

Anchor: Do you think that's happened? Do you think that there's been some irresponsible reporting?

Smith: I wouldn't say irresponsible, I'd say too quick to judge, too quick to say this is what happened – it was civilians in a shelter. I could lay out at least six alternative things that happened there that need to be examined. I think there's too quick judgement on many of these issues to the advantage of Saddam Hussein in many cases.

Gelb: I think the General has an important point there Jim. Because we're in a way too quick to believe our eyes. We see the pictures of this bombed-out facility; we're told it's a shelter. We see bodies which are not in uniform, bodies of people which are not in uniform. And we're told these are civilians and this was a totally civilian operation. And because that's what we see we tend to believe it. There are other explanations that I find just as plausible. So we do have to be especially careful, particularly on a story about killing civilians.

Anchor: What's the alternative, Les?

Gelb: I think the alternative is to present stories like this with appropriate scepticism. We need to make clear at the outset that it has not been established that it's a civilian shelter. And it certainly hasn't been established in any way that we bombed it thinking it was.

Anchor: Les Gelb, do you believe that this could be looked back upon as, could be, could develop into a watershed event in this Persian Gulf War?

Gelb: I don't think so. Because particularly with discussions like these you have a chance to explain to the American people that what they saw may not be what reality was. And by our explaining the other possibilities that it would put it in perspective. And I think there is enough understanding, as the General pointed out, of the vagaries and tragedies of war, that once it's clear we were not targeting civilians, that this was something that happened that we deeply regret. It will not turn out to be a watershed.

Figure 6 Extract from studio discussion, *The MacNeil/Lehrer News Hour*, PBS, broadcast 14 February 1991

implies is an obvious and immediate interpretation of the TV images, that this was a civilian shelter. This speculation and counter-speculation from the talking heads produces a sceptical discourse that functions to keep the bombing of Amiriya within the dominant US narrative that 'the war is going well'. Even within the context of this more analytical genre of news programming, the studio talk neutralizes the debate (i.e. constructs the possibility of this being a civilian shelter as feeding Iraqi propaganda) and restricts space for the testing of the mostly unspoken critique of the whole discourse of 'smart' weaponry upon which the Gulf War was legitimized and fought.

The Iraqis' response to the bombing was to lift all their usual reporting restrictions so that the world's media had unfettered access to its aftermath. In this respect images from this incident could have derailed support for the war in the USA and in other countries contributing to the Coalition, and drawn sympathy in the wider world. Philip M. Taylor (1995), for example, argues: 'In the space between the reality of war and the media image of war, it was the defining moment. For the first time, the Iraqis had the kind of images which fuelled their belief in the Vietnam syndrome – all the more effective for them being taken by western, rather than Iraqi, television crews.'[34] However, the self-censorship applied by the Western media lessened the impact of these images, for their 'standards of taste and decency militated against their full use' (ibid.).

REMEMBERING AMIRIYA

The Iraqis have transformed the place of the death and destruction at Amiriya into a site of remembrance. The shelter has since been transformed into a place 'full' of memory in a number of ways. Firstly, the Iraqis have preserved the remains of the shelter, the impact of one of the two US bombs dropped on it being evident by a hole in the concrete roof and the twisted metal which reinforced it. Secondly, it has been turned into a shrine to those civilians killed in the bombing, with photographs and possessions representing those who had died at this location. Thirdly, other fixtures have been introduced to provide easier access and to mark the site as a significant historical site, in effect as a museum. The result (exactly as the Iraqi Government intended) is unquestionably a site of reflection, of focus on the consequences of the Coalition bombing.

The location of key places of history and memory is often attributed public significance in this way. Places of war and of human suffering particularly are often preserved or marked to provide spaces of continuous remembrance. The notion of the permanence of the past being tied to place is directly related to the fact that memory is a temporal phenomenon. Urry (as noted in Chapter 1) identifies spaces which have been designed as sites for spending time, rather than merely 'passing through'. He argues: 'This seems to presuppose a glacial sense of time, to feel the weight of history, of all the memories of *that* place, and to believe that it will still be there in its essence in many generations time' (1994: 140). For Urry, 'glacial time' is antithetical to the 'placelessness' of the instantaneous time of the media (2002: 158). In respect of Amiriya, the construction of a shrine to those who died there indicates the fragility of our mediated experiences of events in being unable to convey much beyond snapshots of time and to access and sustain a memory of place (even though television news is obsessed with the use of place as an anchor point for stories of events past as well as those unfolding in the present).

Those journalists who were witnesses to atrocities or their aftermath, such as at Amiriya do, however, carry with them the more tangible memory of place. This memory is used to authenticate their later reporting of connected stories and particularly in revisiting the site of the original story. The BBC correspondent Jeremy Bowen, for example, a Coalition pool reporter who visited the original scene of destruction, revisited the Amiriya shelter site as part of a 'special report' for the BBC's *9 O'Clock News* in 1998. His reporting is based upon his personal experience of being present at the original scene:

> I went back to the shelter at Amiriya in Baghdad's western suburbs. When I first came here on a cold morning during the Gulf War seven-and-a-half years ago, rescue workers were taking out the bodies of 403 civilians, who'd just been killed in an American air raid. The West said it was an Iraqi military command centre – I saw no evidence of that. All I found back then were the bodies of women, children and old men. Their pictures line the walls. The shelter has been preserved as their memorial almost exactly as it was when they were killed. (*BBC1*, 9 O'Clock News, *13 July 1998*)

The common practice of television news in revisiting or updating a news story is also to provide visual anchorage or point of reference drawn either from the history of the event, or from another similar event through the use of templates, as I discussed at length in Chapter 2.

Bowen's report, however, contains neither visual material from the Gulf War, nor scenes of the aftermath of the bombing at Amiriya. Perhaps this absence is a reflection of US/UK sensibilities with regard to this incident even after several years. Moreover, the report is shot mostly from the point-of-view of the narrator and this focus on the speaker's perceptual field and the sombre tone of his reporting emphasizes Bowen's personal reflections based upon his being a witness to the aftermath of the bombing. So, although journalistic oral histories are often combined with visual images of that history, in this example, the shelter bombing is powerfully *re-imagined* through the combination of personal memory and the location of reporting. Yet, it is the preserved shelter that conveys an unchanging sense of 'glacial time', to return to Urry's term above. And, as a physical artefact of the past, it seems out-of-sync with the temporalities and the 'emptying' of place that remain synonymous with much of the mediated Gulf War.

SHOWING OR SAVING BODIES? THE ETHICS OF INTERVENTION

The role of journalists in communicating events and circumstances of human suffering and death has always been subject to questions relating to impartiality and ethics. The converse of a 'disowning of injury' is, presumably, the full implication of the human body subject to the consequences of catastrophe or war. Yet, both Western broadcasters and audiences are not prepared to show/be shown graphic images that are not edited and not sanitized. In relation to the Amiriya bombing, Philip M. Taylor (ibid.) argues that 'most editorial rooms bred on a western tradition realised that they would have to take out the graphic close-up images of horribly burned children prior to transmission. They would not show comparable images of a motorway crash or air disaster, so why should war be any different?' Television news in the West tends to be self-regulating in the application of 'standards of taste and decency', with various bodies and mechanisms in different countries responsible for upholding these, although often retrospectively. Yet, as I have suggested, different sensitivities (and standards) are applied in different circumstances and at different times. One enduring contradiction in the application of these emerges between what is deemed showable in fictional representations, and that of actual warfare and catastrophe depicted as 'news'. Martin Bell (1998), the former BBC war correspondent and champion of a journalistic ethics, argues:

> We refuse to show the world as it is. We not only sanitise it but I think to some extent we glorify it because it is not shown in its true horror and therefore people take it as an acceptable way of settling differences. Now that's not just a matter of good and bad taste, that's a matter of right and wrong.[35]

Bell's contribution to this debate stands out from much of the media's self-reflections on these matters in his plain speaking. He presents himself as representative of a shift that has occurred in contemporary journalism from a long BBC tradition of 'detached' and 'objective' reporting which he retrospectively calls 'bystanders' journalism' (1998: 15). In its place, Bell advocates the practice of a 'journalism of attachment', that is: 'a journalism that cares as well as knows; that is aware of its responsibilities; that will not stand neutrally between good and evil, right and wrong, the victim and the oppressor' (1998: 16). In respect of the Gulf War, this description is not readily applicable to much of the material that was actually broadcast in the West during this period, notably in the apparent distance between 'the war' and those journalists reporting it.

Since 1991, however, there has occurred a recognizable shift if not in the nature of images used in the Western media, then at least in the broader strategies in attempting to communicate the realities of human suffering as a consequence of warfare and catastrophe. This shift may not be a conscious path chosen by broadcasters and editors, but rather as a result of the significant increase in the number of news outlets and the consequent increased pressure of competition. On the one hand, this has led to an increase in 'picture clusters' (MacGregor, 1997: 152, see also Chapter 5), with broadcasters and the print media showing very similar images of the same event (for example, the Amiriya bombing in 1991 and the toppling of Saddam's statue in 2003). On the other, journalists and cameramen continue to risk their own lives to show the deadly realities of conflict, in Israel, Somalia, Iraq, and elsewhere.[36] In these circumstances and where the portability of recording and transmitting equipment enables greater proximity to human injury, as-it-happens, news workers are faced with more frequent dilemmas as to whether to continue documenting an atrocity or catastrophe, or to intervene to potentially save lives. In doing so, they may be judged to have compromised journalistic 'standards' of objectivity and impartiality and so risk being prevented from accessing other sites of conflict by those who fear their intervention.

On 10 April 2003, two days after the declared end of the Iraq War, *Channel 4 News'* headline story detailed the unintended shooting of Iraqi civilians by 'jumpy' US marines following a gun battle whilst searching for Saddam and his sons in the Adhamiyah Palace in northern Baghdad. The programme's anchor John Snow introduces the film report: 'Our diplomatic correspondent, Lindsey Hilsum, chanced upon the scene. Her harrowing report contains disturbing images':

Hilsum: We heard periodic shots from the American snipers above [on rooftops, shots audible] their warning to drivers to stop the car. But some people don't understand and speed up. A blue Volkswagen passed. A few minutes later we realized the car which followed had been hit. The marines wouldn't cross into enemy territory but our translator Mohammed Fatnan insisted on going to investigate.

Thank goodness he did. As he ran back towards us we realized that something terrible had happened.

Six-year-old Zara Abdel Samia had been in the back of the car that was shot. She had a head wound. As the marines cleaned up her injury we learned that her aunt and the driver were also injured. (*Extract from* Channel 4 News, *10 April 2003*)

The film report shows Hilsum's translator dressed in a flak jacket, with 'TV' printed in big white letters on front and back, and helmet, walking across an empty street to a car and then running back with the injured girl in his arms and passing her into the arms of another one of the TV crew identified in the same way. These shots are intercut with images of a marine sat on what appears to be an armoured vehicle looking out onto a street and mosque. This accentuates the role played by the television team in rescuing a wounded child whilst the marines literally 'looked on'. Later in the same programme, Hilsum provides a live update from Baghdad and explains that the Americans often use their translator to liaise with the Iraqis, not having one of their own. Again this is an example of media on-the-ground shaping the actions of their subject matter, in this example through the aiding of military communications.

The entire report from Baghdad situates the *Channel 4 News* team as central not only to the story being reported as news, but to its *outcome* in respect of the removal of the injured girl to a place of relative safety and the enabling of medical treatment. Hilsum goes further, however, in using their (TV) actions to justify the continued filming of the story when the Americans object: 'They [US marines] did not want us to film. We pointed out that *they* had shot her. And it was only because of Mohammed that they had any chance of saving her now.' These remarks draw a simplistic contrast between the inaction of the Americans and the willingness of the television crew in attempting to save a child's life. Moreover, the marines' point-of-view is not represented in the report other than Hilsom stating that they 'wouldn't cross into enemy territory'. This provides part of a reason, but hardly constitutes an explanation. For example, the lives of the Americans may have been at grave risk if they had crossed the open street in broad daylight to investigate the car at which they had shot. Further blame is attached to the marines in this and the later live report through speculation that a more effective means of engagement with potential enemies may have prevented this shooting.

In addition to the immediate intervention of media workers on-the-ground in saving victims of war and catastrophe and the shaping of news stories around their actions, often a single injured body is used to focus reporting in representing the suffering of the many. As with the *Channel 4 News* report above, the injuring of a child (who immediately connotes 'innocent civilian' by virtue of their age and thus greater vulnerability than an adult) is often made the central subject. The print media in particular construct campaigns around the personalization of a single victim and in doing so reflexively present themselves as influencing their fate. In the Iraq War, for example, 11-year-old Iraqi Ali Ismaeel Abbas received horrific burns injuries, lost both his arms and was orphaned in a coalition missile strike on Bahgdad. He became the focus of the *Daily Mirror*'s 'Appeal for Ali' 'to help the child victims of war' and to pay for the boy's treatment in Kuwait. The *Mirror* (16 April 2003: 1) reported that Ali had been airlifted out after being 'driven through cheering crowds to a waiting helicopter' under the front-page headline 'HE'S OUT!'. The report describes the newspaper's influence in Ali's rescue: 'Tony Blair asked the US to provide a mercy airlift after reading a heart-rending appeal for help from Ali's nurse in Monday's Mirror' (ibid.). Several months later Ali was flown to Britain for more specialist care.

However, the celebratization of Ali raises concerns as to the nature and effects of the media magnet around one individual. Gaby Hinsliff, in the *Observer*, for example, argues: 'Ali's case prompts wider questions about the morality of plunging one child, however deserving, into a media circus. With at least three newspapers launching rival appeals to rescue him, there were accounts of unseemly scrabbling by reporters over the boy's bedside' (10 August 2003). In this way, the exposure of one injured body skews perspectives of those in the media (desperate not to miss out on being part of the story) and those who watch (through the war and the actions of key players being reduced to simplistic frames of reference in terms of the plight and welfare of one child).

The reflexive interventions of the news media in events they cover assign them greater responsibility in determining outcomes. This is so both in respect of the immediacy and proximity to the injured body (afforded through technological advances in broadcasting) and in the 'adopting' of a single child or incident to direct audiences' responses to a cause with which newspapers or programmes can associate themselves. In these circumstances journalists will often be caught in a dilemma of mixed motives between saving lives and *being seen* to save lives.

FADING IMAGES?

As noted at the opening of this chapter, audiences can now tune in to a niche version of warfare that allows them more easily to opt out of a global consciousness and memory of suffering. However, at the same time, certain news programmes and newspapers have developed reputations based upon a critical journalism that attempts to engage with the horrific consequences of waging war. The *Independent*'s coverage of the Iraq War, for example, rather than employing images of the dead and injured across its front page, instead occasionally filled much of this space with extraordinarily graphic printed descriptions of events, notably from correspondent Robert Fisk reporting from Baghdad. On 27 March 2003, for example, the proportion of its front page devoted to printed words compared with images across the front cover of this broadsheet was around 90 per cent. This can be seen in contrast to the more usual bold headline and image(s) accounting for around half of the front page of tabloid newspapers. The top story on this day was the killing of Iraqi civilians by two missiles from an American jet landing in a crowded Baghdad marketplace. The printed words of Fisk's report are set out in a column that runs the entire width of the page, covering over half of it, before being split amongst several columns further down. Three photographs from the aftermath of the bombing are reproduced in colour on the same page, but only as relatively small insets, and the words of the report are afforded greater visual impact than the pictures. Their content is also explicit:

It was an outrage, an obscenity. The severed hand on the metal door, the swamp of blood and mud across the road, the human brains inside a garage, the incinerated, skeletal remains of an Iraqi mother and her three small children in their still-smouldering car.

By way of contrast, the *Independent*'s competitor – the *Guardian* – on the same day carried a front-page photograph of the bloodied body of an Iraqi man caught in the bombing surrounded by shocked onlookers. This image and the accompanying headline 'Wayward Bombs Bring Marketplace Carnage' occupied a similar proportion of space to the main text of Fisk's report on the same story.

One explanation for the *Independent*'s strategy, other than its adoption of a strong anti-war position, is to visually contrast with its picture-driven competitors on the news-stand. Moreover, with readerships accustomed to images of the dead and dying on their front pages from war zones and sites of catastrophe around the globe, as I have noted, these images can lose their force over time. In our image-saturated environment of stock images and picture clusters, occasionally shifting the balance of headline news away from the picture and onto a more graphic text in the written word may actually be more shocking and more provocative.

The explicitness of the *Independent*'s written discourse provides a sharp contrast to the reporting of the marketplace bombing across much of the rest of the British media. By contrast, in the Middle East, where government censorship restricts much of what can be written in the daily press, there was an inversion of the reporting of the *Independent*. As Raban (2003: 4) observes of the *Jordan Times* and other newspapers in the region, 'photographs could afford to be more eloquent and candid than the stories printed beneath them'. These culturally- and geographically-specific differing strategies in reporting the carnage of the Iraq War demonstrate elements of a 'journalism of attachment' that offer at least some alternatives to the sanitized and sanitizing perspectives that dominate much of the American-owned or influenced mass media.

A potential problem with the distinctive and I think successful approach of the *Independent* in its occasional use of the printed word over the photographic image is that it is precisely the latter, as I have explored in previous chapters, that tends to endure in memory over the former. In this way, although the marketplace bombing has yet to emerge in a history of the Iraq War not as yet written, its resonance in a Western-mediated memory may be disproportionately less than stories in which visual images actually defined news content. However, unless a truly remarkable image emerges from this story (one that is distinctive and simply more memorable), images of the injured and the dead may simply merge with those of the many other incidents of war casualties into a faded mediated memory of the Iraq War. In this respect, the written word may (and as a front-page image in itself) come to define the story.

To consider this point further, we may consider the representation of those images from the aftermath of the war which were deemed as instantly iconic. In late July 2003, the US search for members of the former Iraqi regime finally produced Saddam Hussein's sons, Uday and Qusay. Both were killed in a six-hour gun battle when troops besieged the brothers' hideout in Mosul in northern Iraq. There appeared to be some debate within the US administration as to the merits or otherwise of releasing photographs of their bodies to the world's media. However, this was probably inevitable, being the only assured way of convincing the world (and particularly Iraqis) that Saddam's former henchmen were indeed dead and unable to reassert their ruthless grip on power over Iraq. Four photographs showing the bloodstained and contorted faces of the brothers were released by the Americans on 24 July and were carried by most of the visual media around the globe. A number of tabloid and other newspapers filled their front pages and employed demonizing headlines more commonly associated with Saddam and inviting readers to look at more of the images inside. The *Daily Mirror* 'THE EVIL DEAD – Report and more shocking pictures: pages 4 & 5' (Figure 7) is typical in this respect.

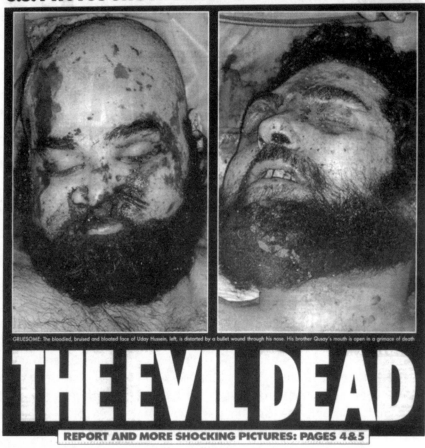

Figure 7   The *Daily Mirror*, 25 July 2003

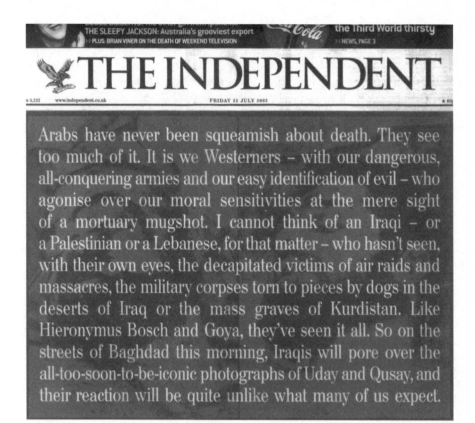

THE SLEEPY JACKSON: Australia's grooviest export   the Third World thirsty
PLUS: BRIAN VINER ON THE DEATH OF WEEKEND TELEVISION   NEWS, PAGE 3

THE INDEPENDENT

www.independent.co.uk   FRIDAY 25 JULY 2003

Arabs have never been squeamish about death. They see too much of it. It is we Westerners – with our dangerous, all-conquering armies and our easy identification of evil – who agonise over our moral sensitivities at the mere sight of a mortuary mugshot. I cannot think of an Iraqi – or a Palestinian or a Lebanese, for that matter – who hasn't seen, with their own eyes, the decapitated victims of air raids and massacres, the military corpses torn to pieces by dogs in the deserts of Iraq or the mass graves of Kurdistan. Like Hieronymus Bosch and Goya, they've seen it all. So on the streets of Baghdad this morning, Iraqis will pore over the all-too-soon-to-be-iconic photographs of Uday and Qusay, and their reaction will be quite unlike what many of us expect.

Figure 8   The *Independent*, 25 July 2003

The *Independent* of the same day also reproduced photographs of the heads of Uday and Qusay Hussin on its front page. However, it super-imposes a red screen and white words over the top of the images so that they are barely distinguishable (Figure 8). The content of the text over the images argues that Iraqis (and many others) live in environments in which they have become anaesthetized to death and are unlikely to be moved by the pictures. This contrasts with Western 'moral sensitivities' over images of the dead in a culture that simplifies the nature of 'evil' through the waging of war. Despite the unambiguous use of the photo-graphs by the tabloids, these sensitivities were evident in other British media. For example, *The Times'* front page carried an enlarged image in colour showing part of the face of Uday Hussein, whilst a photograph of the head of each brother was printed deep inside the newspaper in black-and-white. Perhaps somewhat disingenously, *The Times* cautions its readers as to their nature: 'The photographs are reproduced on page 15, readers may find them disturbing.'

The photographs of the dead sons of Saddam Hussein are significant to the portrayal and memory of the Iraq War in their instant iconization. Their explicit nature (in terms of Western visual news media) and the controversy over their use contributed to their impact. For instance, wide dissemination of these photographs was in direct contradiction to the fierce denouncing of Al-Jazeera's showing of dead and captured American soldiers by the USA and their media only four months earlier. The *Independent*'s use of them, however, serves to close down the images themselves and instead produces a more critical and reflexive discourse on their release by the Americans and their reproduction in the media and Western responses to this.

British and particularly American television news could also be accused of hypocrisy over their differential treatment of images of dead Westerners released by the Iraqis compared with their showing of the scarred faces of the dead Hussein brothers. *Channel 4 News*, however, did provide some historical context with Jon Snow (the programme's main anchor) describing the release and dissemination of these photographs as 'a global version of a head on a spike' (24 July 2003). The same programme used visual templates to produce a history of the parading of the bodies of enemies and dictators in a report entitled 'Picturing the Enemy', before which Snow cautions, 'The following images are of corpses which some of you may find disturbing' (ibid.). These included: Mussolini and his mistress strung up above a crowded square in 1945; the executed Ceausescu and his wife, 1989; Pol Pot in Cambodia, 1998; and US soldiers after being dragged through the streets of Mogadishu, Somalia, 1993. The fifth template was the example of Al-Jazeera footage of dead Americans shown first on Iraqi TV in March 2003. However, these images were not included in this report but were merely described (instead Al-Jazeera pictures of Iraqis waving weapons in a street were shown) with Snow acknowledging their absence by reminding viewers: 'Many broadcasters in Europe chose not to show the unedited video' (ibid.). The omission of these images is indicative of the still relatively short body lag since the time of the killing of these US soldiers. Originally, as noted earlier, *Channel 4 News* did not broadcast the film of the captured and dead Americans, but instead showed a still image of each of the POWs.

The photographs of the bloodied faces of Uday and Qusay Hussein offer what is likely to become an enduring contradiction in the new memory of the Iraq War. As future media templates of their own, it is difficult to imagine them other than iconic images of the war (and its aftermath) given their graphic (and thus memorable) nature *and* extremely extensive dissemination across the visual mass media. When an image becomes the story it is even more likely to eclipse others and, as Sontag (2003: 89) argues, 'The problem is not that people remember through photographs, but that they remember only through the photographs' (ibid.). The *Independent* coverage considered here is an exception in its attempt to provide a more critical discourse in its use and commentary on these images. However, both in terms of news and memory, the iconic image is difficult to resist, and although it may be subverted or altered in our intensely visual history and culture (as with the *Independent* treatment), it is the iconic that endures. The selection and use of images of war by the media may at times be a haphazard process but, increasingly, it is snared in the very story frame it itself is constructing. In the case of the photographs of the Hussein brothers, US propaganda was directly served by their mass dissemination. Whether a meaningful and critical narrative can be produced that competes with these images and their anchorage of a mediated memory of the Iraq War and its aftermath remains to be seen.

Chapter 5

The real Saddam?

MONSTER OR MISJUDGED?

Whereas the images of Uday and Qusay Hussein became globally iconic in death, rather than in life, they remain eclipsed by the living image of their father. 'Saddam', as the former Iraqi president is known (denoting a universal familiarity appropriate for a demon), casts a large and enduring shadow, and not least over three successive US presidents (and the same number of British prime ministers). Yet his worldwide notoriety is probably the most disproportionate of any leader in modern history.

His brutality as President, his invasion of Iran in 1980 and subsequent eight-year war, and his use of poison gas against the Kurds in Halabja in 1988 (see Chapter 2) were all of no great surprise to his people, despite the suffering and deaths. Meanwhile, the West during this period did not intervene against Saddam, and not least as the suppression of Iran was considered to be in their interests. The Western response to Saddam's invasion and annexing of Kuwait in 1990 is, then, perhaps even more surprising. Although there was some agreement (in the West, not in the Middle East) that action needed to be taken, it was the discourse justifying this action that afforded Saddam a new global status as demon. Brian Walden (1998) points out that at this time, 'nothing was said about Saddam Hussein being a small time local criminal, the emphasis was ever more luridly placed on an entirely different concept – that Saddam was a super-human monster who threatened the peace of the entire world and the security of everybody in it'.[37] The simplicity of the idea of Saddam as an unpredictable madman with further expansionist aims for Iraq was one easily sold by politicians and readily reproduced in the media. However, the establishing of the Iraqi leader's notoriety should be viewed firmly in the context of the coinciding period of mass expansion in global electronic news media, notably from 1990 to the present day.

He is probably the most demonized leader of the television age but also one whose own use of television often gifted propaganda to the West. From the display of his greeting the so-called 'human shields' in August 1990 through to images of the captured Coalition pilots in January 1991 and captured and dead Americans in March 2003, there appeared a series of misjudgements in his use of television, if courting world opinion was ever his aim. The globally-iconized visual image of Saddam was that which was lifted from Iraq TV broadcasts. These defined the dictator in various guises, often in military uniform, presiding over meetings of his officials, and being enthusiastically received by the Iraqi public. However, the Iraq War witnessed another jump in the Western demonizing rhetoric almost to the extent that its effect was nullified. That is to say, Saddam's frequent visual construction as a pariah on our TV screens, particularly from 1990 onwards, had afforded him a certain familiarity that significantly de-mystified the demon. The 'superhuman monster' rhetoric appeared to unravel as the political argument for invading Iraq met with considerable opposition outside of the USA. Instead, Saddam managed to maintain his grip on power as the West obsessed over the elusive Weapons of Mass Destruction (WMDs) and the intangible 'Regime'.

The image of Saddam had been so thoroughly mediated over this period that he appeared increasingly as an enemy of history (of 1990 to be precise) rather than one of the present and the future as proclaimed by George Bush and Tony Blair. Although there is much film footage recorded and broadcast of the former Iraqi President over many years prior to his capture, the enduring mediated memory of Saddam was mostly derived from relatively few images which reinforced simplistic Western political representations. This involved the repeated use of 'stock' images of Saddam inserted into the 'mix' of live and other TV coverage.

One of the consequences of the dominance of stock images is that through their instant, repetitious and global dissemination they may inhibit access to alternative frames of reference for audiences. The propaganda potential for the use of stock images can increase during times of collective unease and particularly in times of war. Stock images are significant in view of their familiarity for audiences, and yet this very familiarity can also act to provide resistance to critical reading by reinforcing the stereotypes conveyed through or associated with those images. Yet in the visually-saturated media environment of today, familiarity can soon develop into fatigue. As noted in Chapter 2, Sontag argues, 'An image is drained of its force by the way it is used, where and how often it is seen. Images shown on television are by definition images of which, sooner or later, one tires' (2003: 105). In this way the once powerfully demonizing representations of Saddam appeared to lose their impact, through their remediation and repetition over time, eventually even undermining the political and mediated justification for the US/UK invasion of Iraq in 2003.

There are three key issues in relation to the impact of stock images: firstly, they are infrequently dated, so that audiences can be oblivious as to the time and context of their recording; secondly, their very repetition acts reflexively to promote their recognition and even greater circulation (i.e. they are used precisely because they are instantly recognizable); and, thirdly and relatedly, they may bare little or no resemblance to what or whom they depict today. In this respect, stock images constitute a false media memory. They represent a past without signifying it as past.

This chapter explores the mechanisms through which stock images of and other discourses on the Iraqi President became established in the media coverage of the West's wars against Iraq. This involves examination of representations of Saddam in both enhancing and eventually weakening support for military action against him. I trace the rise and fall of the demonized image of Saddam Hussein as imposed and later over-imposed by the West as assisted through the iconic fixations of the media. Support for action in the Gulf on a number of occasions from 1991 to 2003 has been aided by an over-simplistic Western media representation of Saddam – a view that has also been drawn upon by Hollywood and television drama. In these circumstances, the Western dominant cultural memory of Saddam has already been forged and that media (or 'popular') history increasingly influences 'professional' history, in its highly selective, repetitive and pervasive modes of representation.

Saddam's creation of a public image culture pervaded by signs of himself (e.g. paintings, statues and televised walkabouts) inevitably fed Western visual representations. The enemy was personified in the evil, ruthless Iraqi leader in US and UK political and news discourses to an intensity that increased his standing in the Middle East and in the wider world far beyond the real threat he posed. Walden (1998) for example, argued, somewhat prophetically:

> Look what our demonisation of him has led to. It's an extraordinary story. That so much suffering, so much human and material cost could have been inflicted upon the world by somebody who's little more than a bandit chief is amazing. Here we stand: with all our technology, with our computers and our smart bombs and our global economy. And there he stands: a creature almost of another world leading a shambles of a country which has never been able to solve any of its fundamental problems. And yet he manages to come out on top. Why? Because we refused to accept the complexities of the real world and understand them, and decided to impose upon events the stirring simplicities of a Hollywood action film. We've done it before, and we shall probably do it again.[38]

The image of Saddam as monster and villain was simply not sustainable over the period 1990–2003. The acclaimed defeat of Saddam in respect of the liberation of Kuwait in 1991 slowly unravelled as he alone was constructed as *the* enemy and so his retention of power afforded him the status of victor. The finality of the outcome of the Gulf War in this respect became increasingly ambiguous through the 1990s as he adopted a strategy of brinksmanship with the USA in attempting to outmanoeuvre United Nations weapons inspectors.

However, in relation to new sources of terror emerging to threaten the West (e.g. Milosevic in Europe and bin Laden in the USA), Saddam appeared as an increasingly peripheral figure. The attempt to re-establish him as an immediate and serious threat by Bush (and Blair) as part of the declared 'War on Terror' (after the attacks of September 11, 2001) presented a considerable discursive challenge. Saddam the tyrant was simply old news and old memory, mostly constructed from what was or what looked like old footage; aged over the thirteen years his presence in the West (remediated from Iraqi TV) appeared to be from a different era. Iraq's WMD capability of '45 minutes' listed amongst other justifications for the Iraq War in a UK Government 'dossier' looked out-of-sync with the Saddam on screen. Particularly in the build-up to and during the Iraq War he appeared almost as a caricature of himself, the only and ultimate template used in the media. And, as the war progressed, TV channels ran biographies of Saddam, as though they were obituaries, pre-empting his last stand in Baghdad. The combination of the failing rhetoric about him and the inevitability of his fall from power paradoxically diminished his demonic status and functioned to make the Iraq War more difficult to sell. It is to the success and ultimate failure of the simplistic mediated representations of Saddam used by successive US Presidents to justify years of hostility and conflict against Iraq that I now turn. How central were the media in the construction of Saddam Hussein as a world-threatening tyrant from 1990 and then in the literal toppling of the image they had helped to create, over a decade later?

'GUEST'S NEWS'

The familiar image of Saddam Hussein in military attire appearing on Iraqi TV inspecting his armies or presiding over his version of cabinet was put into contrast by footage broadcast on 23 August 1990 of him in a smart civilian suit sitting amongst over twenty Westerners, including children. This was the same month in which Iraq had invaded and annexed Kuwait, and a number of Westerners unlucky enough to have been stranded in Baghdad had been detained. They were in effect deployed as 'human shields' against the threat of retaliation for Iraq's action in Kuwait with some being held at sites of likely key targets; Saddam, however, insisted they be described as 'prevention' rather than as a 'shield', as he played 'host' to his 'guests'. Indeed, every morning the Iraqis telexed CNN listing that day's schedule on Iraqi TV which included *Guest's News* (Rosenberg, 1990: 1). This 45-minute programme proved the first real 'hit' of the conflict on TV and CNN put it out on air the moment they received it (as they did with a lot of pool footage supplied by the Pentagon during the war itself).

As either a threat to the potential consequences of a Western attack or as a piece of 'charm' propaganda, the screening of the hostages with Saddam spectacularly backfired. The Iraqi President explained through an interpreter to his 'guests' the reasons for their internment and even asked them questions, although barely pausing to allow for their responses. The whole scene was surreal and even ended with a 'group' photograph and Saddam shaking the hands of his 'guests', as though he was hosting his own TV chat show. All that was absent was the studio audience and the end rolling credits. Wark (1994: 3–4) describes this genre-breaking performance:

> Looking like a cross between Bob Hope and Geraldo Rivera, Saddam appeared to Western viewers as a demented talk-show host, in gross breach of the etiquette even of 'reality television', where only crooks, pimps, prostitutes, and unscrupulous used-car salesmen may be treated to raw acts of intimate verbal violence on camera. Or perhaps the format of the programme looked uncomfortably close to Oprah Winfrey on a bad day, talking about bondage or child abuse.

The familiarity and safety of the TV environment simply projected an image of Saddam as conman; viewers could not easily accept the perceptual leap in representation and rhetoric from murderous dictator to paternal host. The credibility gap was such that commentators reflected on the Iraqi leader's extreme misjudgement in misreading Western audiences' responses. Others compared him with evil leaders from history, Walter Goodman (1990: 11), for example, reflects, 'Where had we seen such a performance before? Perhaps it was the moustache and the children, but wasn't there a resemblance to Uncle Joe Stalin playing Mr Nice Guy?'

Politicians on both sides of the Atlantic reacted with horror. The British Foreign Secretary Douglas Hurd, for example, was widely cited: 'I hold it as the most sickening thing I've seen in a long time. I think the manipulation of children in that sort of way is contemptible' (CBS *Morning News*, 24 August 1990). The footage from Iraqi TV that seemed to provoke the greatest revulsion included Saddam tousling the hair of some of the young children, playing with familial intimacy the role of grandfather. One image in particular soon became a symbol of the outrage voiced through the media in the West, appearing in news programmes and on the front pages the following day. This depicted Saddam patting the head and holding the arm of a British boy, seven-year-old Stuart Lockwood. However, the misjudgement of this display by Saddam and his officials can be seen in relation to the anticipated response of the Iraqi people, as Akbar Ahmed observes: 'In his culture an elder, or figure of authority, often displays affection to children by patting the child or tousling the hair. It is socially approved and appreciated' (cited in Wark, 1994: 5). This places some of the British and US responses into quite a different context, exposing them as ignorant or at least as over-simplistic framings which perpetuated the image of Saddam as demon being rapidly forged by the West at this time. Whether Saddam himself was ever made aware of how his performance played out beyond the Middle East and to what extent his political isolation was matched with isolation from the globally reflexive TV event he was featuring in is unclear. What is apparent, however, is that the image of him with Stuart Lockwood became a key component in the demonizing narrative that pervaded the media coverage of the war.

For example, to return to the aftermath of the bombing of the Amiriya bunker on 13 February 1991 (see Chapter 4), the USA used Saddam's placing of human shields at military installations as an immediate explanation for the civilian casualties inflicted at Amiriya. The White House spokesman, Marlin Fitzwater, employed this direct comparison in a briefing the day after the bunker bombing. In a report showing excerpts from his speech, CBS imported visual stills taken from archived television footage to accompany the audio of Fitzwater's account of Saddam's actions involving placing civilians in harm's way. His briefing is part-statement, part-conjecture:

> Civilian hostages were moved in November and December to military sites for use as human shields.
>
> POWs reportedly having been placed at military sites.
>
> Command and control centres have been placed on top of schools and public buildings.
> (*Marlin Fitzwater,* White House Briefing, *CBS, 14 February 1991*)

However, it is the visual footage and stills that impose a convincing narrative, neatly connecting images of the bruised (i.e. beaten) captured Coalition pilots, Saddam holding the arm of Stuart Lockwood, and a building. The latter is not recognizable as a 'command and control centre' nor is its vicinity to a 'school' or 'public building' clear, yet this image still serves to authenticate Fitzwater's account, thereby contributing to a much more convincing comparison. The obvious reason that networks provide visual illustration to talk on television is that it is simply more interesting to watch such images than to watch a speaker sitting in the studio or standing (as with Fitzwater) at a podium in the White House press room. Yet, whereas many reputable news organizations and programmes attempt to provide a balance in spoken debate, their use of visual images to illustrate that debate is often taken as more transparent, and particularly in the daily use of stock pictures. The mixing of quickly-retrievable archive footage to forge instant visual narratives is a standard feature of television news today (as I explored in Chapter 2). However, in the coverage of the White House briefing above, CBS are in effect doing the work of Fitzwater by following his words with images. These images (as with other US networks during the Gulf War) were rebroadcast in other countries, with this CBS coverage being carried with subtitles by TF1 in France, for example. And it is this unequivocal visual media imaging of Saddam and his actions that can be seen as central to the effective Western demonization of him throughout much of the 1990s.

The Coalition POW footage was edited down to mostly the key stills that I have identified as later templates used in coverage of the Iraq War, and the 45 minutes of the forerunner to Saddam's *Guest's News* were reduced to an iconic image of Saddam and Stuart Lockwood.[39] These emergent frames of the 1991 Gulf War primarily served to anchor media and political representations of the Iraqi President in a context of evil to an extent that there were few alternative visions of him available. However, it is the use of mediated images of Saddam himself and their repetition that has driven his iconic presence in the West into history itself.

THE OLD SADDAM

There are a number of enduring stock television images of Saddam that have been repeated since (and are part of) his rise on the world stage from around 1990. An oft-repeated scene over this time is an obviously staged walkabout by Saddam over some sand next to an open expanse of water. Dressed in khaki uniform complete with army beret and big shoulder lapels and accompanied by officials all also dressed in military attire, he greets a group of what appear to be army regulars waving rifles and other guns in the air in an aggressive show of support. There is nothing particularly remarkable about this as a standard piece of propaganda film, yet it has become part of the stock Western television imagery on Saddam. Presumably this is because it instantly conveys him as 'military leader' and one who has (or can manage) the command of what appears

Table 5: Use of stock images of Saddam in news reports, trailers and movies

Date	Channel/Movie	Context
19.1.1991	CNN	Part of a CNN trailer promoting their coverage of the Gulf War
14.2.1991	CBS (also relayed by French cable TV)	Story following Amiriya bunker coverage
12.8.1995	CNN	Defection of Saddam's son-in-laws
1996	*Courage Under Fire*	Opening few minutes of movie
12.2.1998	*Channel 4 News*	Blocking access to UNSCOM inspectors to presidential palaces
2001	*Three Kings*	Opening few minutes of movie
20.3.2003	BBC1 *6 O'Clock News*	Part of mini-biography of Saddam

to be a rabble of fighting men, and illustrates stories relating to his characteristic defiance. Stills or excerpts from this footage have been shown on television on many occasions and examples are given in Table 5 to illustrate its different usage as stock news image as well as its use in fictional representations of the Gulf War.

It is the reproduction and reconstruction of the same images interwoven into a present, sometimes part-live, narrative that promotes television as a site of seemingly instant history. This process itself, however, does not require time-consuming searches of archival material, but as noted earlier, is now instantly accessible. For example, in the event of the breaking news of the defection of Saddam's son-in-laws from Iraq, CNN transmitted live a statement by General Hussein Kame declaring this fact on 12 August 1995. By the early evening CNN *World News*, within only a couple of hours of this story breaking, had embedded these stock images of Saddam into its main report. In February 1998, Saddam's cat-and-mouse games with UNSCOM weapons' inspectors resulted in a mainly US and British build-up of forces in the Gulf in preparation for 'Operation Desert Thunder' (as dubbed by President Clinton) against 'military targets' in Iraq. Again the stock image of the strong and the militant Saddam peppered news reports. Meanwhile Clinton, who was threatening Saddam with the unleashing of Desert Thunder, was himself soon haunted by stock news images, notably footage of his public 'embrace' with Monica Lewinsky.[40]

A key problem with 'image histories' of people, places and events is their apparent irrefutability, particularly when strengthened through repetition on TV and remediation across other media. Television is the ideal medium for such constructions as often no further contextualization or explanation is required when an image or set of images supports news narratives or goes beyond that which is more risky to insinuate or suggest in news talk. In terms of communicating news and forging history, as noted earlier in Chapter 1, visual images are massively underrated and provide us with our 'subliminal points of reference', in the words of Samuel (1994: 27). The memory of Clinton's Presidency as forged through television, for example, is literally 'contaminated' by the Lewinsky images that were used repeatedly and effectively in visually contradicting his denials of their affair. But in terms of less news-frenzied times, Samuel's assessment is very perceptive. On the one hand, there are the headline 'flashframes' of memory – the defining visual images of our age that come to anchor the history of events by virtue of their exceptional quality – and on the other, the media provide us with less obvious but nonetheless powerful and enduring images that accumulate in media memory and define not by being extraordinary, but by being ordinary, by 'fitting' and thus reinforcing existing ideas and conceptions.

Of course the former, a flashframe of memory, can soon fade to resemble the latter and be 'drained of its force' (Sontag, 2003) with its repetition and increasing familiarity with audiences. The dominant representations of Saddam (even his televised meeting with the Western hostages) are reduced to disconnected images that have limited resonance (other than through their repetition) with audiences who do not possess living memories of the times and events sown into the patchwork of current news stories. For instance, to employ Neil Postman's well-cited critique of US television news, news presenters and editors themselves are not wholly to blame for its entertainment-driven content, as there exists 'a straightforward recognition that "good television" has little to do with what is "good" about exposition or other forms of verbal communication but everything to do with what the pictorial images look like' (1987: 90). 'Faded' stock images in this way *are* the context for they are often presented without temporal reference or much in the way of verbal explanation. TV news can thus be seen to promote an essentially inhibited and oversimplified view of the past and of people, not just through its paucity of detail and brevity of language, but because it is increasingly dependent upon the visual image for its direction and nar-rative. Such images (as I have indicated with the Saddam-Lockwood frame) provide only flickering memories and are hardly the basis for the construction of a meaningful or substantive past.

However, sometimes these flickering memories are assembled into more coherent and reflective narratives within news programmes or in promotional trailers of coverage (as examined earlier in Chapter 3). At these times, TV's capacity to visualize the past through a montage of fragments is made more obvious. At the height of the Iraq War, when speculation as to Saddam's whereabouts and likely next move was at a peak, BBC1's *6 O'Clock News* ran a two-minute Special Report on Saddam entitled 'Under Siege'. In effect this was a mini-biography com-piled from around a dozen clips from film footage and photographs. The narration provided by Jeremy Bowen is a concisely worded and balanced account outlining Saddam's ruthlessness in having his enemies shot at a Ba'ath Party meeting in 1979, his sons-in-law killed after they returned from defection in 1995, and his use of chemical weapons against Iran and the Kurds in Iraq in the 1980s. Bowen reflects upon the possible sce-narios for Saddam in his current predicament and ends his report: 'Perhaps in his bunker he's hoping for a glorious last stand to make him in death the Arab hero he wanted to be in life' (20 March 2003). Of course this kind of description is in keeping with representations of Saddam as a mythical figure.

The visuals in Bowen's two-minute biography of Saddam Hussein, outlined in Table 6, demonstrate television's capacity for combining frag-ments of diverse images drawn from a range of times to forge a simplis-tic narrative – an instant history of the principal target of the Iraq War. Although Bowen does reference some of the dates and context of the report, much of it is comprised of stock images that are frequently used as templates to frame news stories around Saddam and Iraq. Examples numbered 1, 5 and 11 in Table 6, in particular, refer to footage that could have been drawn from anytime over a decade or more prior to the Iraq War. The footage of Saddam with his 'human shields' (7) is inserted into the middle of this report although Bowen does not mention it, nor is it referenced anywhere else in the report. Audiences with living memory of the time around the 1991 War may recognize this several-second clip or they may be familiar with its use as stock footage; younger viewers may not. For the latter group (and perhaps for much of the audience) these

Table 6: Images used in Jeremy Bowen's report 'Under Siege', *6 O'Clock News*, BBC1, 20 March 2003

	Visuals	Date (if given)	B+W or Colour
1	Streets of Baghdad with shots of walls and buildings adorned with images of Saddam		B+W
2	Very poor quality footage of Ba'ath Party meeting with Saddam speaking and ordering out traitors to be shot	1979	B+W
3	Hussein family photo including sons-in-law		colour
4	Son-in-law addressing media in Jordan after defection	1995	colour
5	Saddam taking seat at head of table with officials		colour
6	Launching of land missiles against Iran by Iraqi army		B+W
7	Saddam in civilian suit with seven-year-old Stuart Lockwood		B+W
8	Saddam with look-alikes (decoys) swimming in river		colour
9	Saddam (or decoy) meeting foreign visitor sitting in opulent setting		colour
10	Excerpt from movie Saddam made of his own failed attempt to kill the then Iraqi President	1959	B+W
11	Saddam in olive-uniform and beret on walkabout with military officials greeting chanting supporters		colour
12	Saddam saluting his armies on parade		colour

images are redundant for they are not placed into their past (and thus significant) context. In this way stock images can be disconnected from that meaning originally afforded to them that may have given rise to their very selection for inclusion in news reports in the first place.

Perhaps in this way Samuel's notion (above) of the visual constituting of 'our stock figures, our subliminal points of reference, our unspoken point of address' (1994: 27) is an entirely appropriate description of the nature and function of these images. That is to say, their circulation in news programmes and elsewhere (i.e. entering fictional accounts as with the stock image of Saddam greeting his supporters) produces 'ambient' memory, namely a memory drawn from pervasive and repetitious media images, a memory that is 'now/here', literally placeless but seen in the here-and-now of news reports. In this way there develops 'a past without a past', one that is not remembered in relation to *why* this image or that image has become a dominant representation of a past event, but where they are recognized or accepted as such.

If visual images are the fundamental base of human memory (as I have argued), then the nature of these images and their circulation pose a fundamental problem for how mediated societies come to 'see' others of whom their society possesses limited cultural knowledge. In such an environment it becomes difficult to identify an 'unpolluted' Saddam, for example, from the demonizing discourse, the dated images, and the numerous talking-head biographers who saturate our media with 'expertise', commenting and speculating on his every move.

Key to the skewed view that constructs a past without a past is that ambient memory tends to 'float free' in the present. In this way, and at the same time, there can be said to occur a 'collapse of memory', for, as Jose M. Arcaya argues, 'remembering' requires the 'rememberer' to unite the 'now' with the 'then':

> For something to be recognized as past, it must be seen not only in terms of its 'thereness' or immediate facticity, but as part of a tradition contextualizing the object within a temporal order of historical happenings and anticipated eventualities. (*1992: 308–9*)

Yet it is precisely this tradition and temporal ordering that television can seemingly mix and subvert as it routinely combines the here with there, the now with then. Television news appears to exercise increasing freedom in employing visual images to illustrate stories and represent people and events without reference, context or caption. The temporality of the medium abrogates much of TV news' responsibility for accounting for its selection, presentation and juxtaposition of images. At least in the print media the reproduction of photographs and stills requires a minimum of captioning; newspaper and magazine images effect a presence that demand explanation and contextualization.

It is the unmarked images of Saddam on TV that contributed to an environment in which discourses attempting to justify action against him (in 1991 in particular) could flourish, and it is to these that I now turn.

FROM 'HITLER' TO 'INSPECTOR CLOUSEAU'

President Bush Snr helped colour much of the media language and debate about the Iraqi President by describing him as 'the Hitler of the '90s' at the beginning of the decade. The problem with this incredible analogy (in addition to being flawed historically) is that it made Saddam appear credible as a *world* player in terms of constituting a threat. Language aside, this was achieved through the disproportionate (in relation to the threat posed) media attention he was afforded, as Elihu Katz (1991: 44) argues: 'The media "decided" that the Gulf crisis should be told as a gladiatorial contest. Since gladiators must be equal opponents or the contest is no fun, the media helped make them so, offering "equal time" to trade public threats and insults while getting ready to fight.' Much of the US TV coverage in 1990–91 treated Saddam's presidential addresses with a similar reverence to those of their own President, at least in trailing and citing from them. Besides, the coverage of the presidential addresses by Saddam offered another feature of the televised conflict that contributed to its liveness (even when not broadcast live), they were often carried in full with spoken English translation. The 'equalizing' of the sides in the 1991 War was achieved by the reflexive TV environment, as well as by press headlines, which instituted a kind of discursive parity between the leader of a superpower and 'the thief of Baghdad'.[41]

The comparisons of Saddam with Hitler became part of heated debates in the media, both following 1990 and even continuing with the outbreak of the Iraq War thirteen years later. A significant problem of this discursive elevation of Saddam to demonic status comparable with Hitler is that its mediated façade was not easily sustainable in an environment where such issues are played out on television but where the visual images are not of the same substance. Shapiro (1997: 77) for example, argues:

> Saddam Hussein, his 'Republican Guards', and the area of the Iraqi troop concentration constituted the bodily and spatial antagonisms of the war. But those bodies and spaces remained relatively nonfigurable and certainly not very palpable as the war was seen through the sighting devices of US weapons during the telecasts of video footage of the war.

The stock ambient images of Saddam that from around 1990 became the standard fare of television news' representations have had a declining correlation to the political rhetoric necessary to engender support for military (and particularly ground) engagement against him. The most commonly used visual images of Saddam tended to fade in their impact as the 1990s progressed. Following his brutal crushing of Kurdish and other resistance (who had been encouraged by the USA to rise against him), few new flashframes emerged to re-ignite world opinion against Saddam. The Republican Guards remained 'nonfigurable', on television at least, even in their defeat in 2003, for they, with Saddam, seemingly 'melted away'.

By the time of the Iraq War, however, not only had the demonization of Saddam via the media become jaded, but there appeared a growing credibility gap between the image(s) and the rhetoric. For example, Fouad Ajami, a Middle East 'expert' speaking on the second Saddam-Clinton crisis of 1998, characterizes this shift in discourses:

> Freud would love this man. I mean there's the whole, you know, we used to say that Saddam is the Hitler of his time, and I always thought that, in a way, Saddam, perhaps, is the Inspector Clouseau of his time. He's a very clumsy man. He's miscalculated before and he will miscalculate now. (*CBS*, This Morning, *13 November 1998*)

Indeed, Saddam's ability to undermine attempts to contain him by forces led by the USA made his outspoken enemies in the most powerful nation in the world look increasingly foolish. As noted earlier, from January of 1998 Clinton's Presidency was suffering the almost daily ridicule of extensive news coverage of his affair and denials of his affair with a White House Intern, Monica Lewinsky. The US media began to openly question Clinton's motives for his increasingly aggressive language and approach towards Saddam. Unfortunately for Clinton, they seized upon a fictional template to frame his apparent shift in rhetoric, namely the movie *Wag the Dog*. This film, on release in the States in this period, depicts a US President going to war with Albania in order to distract public and political attention away from a domestic scandal. The parallels were an opportunity not to be missed by television news and a number of channels ran this template in 1998, including CNN, ABC and NBC. However, the ultimate snub probably came with CNN's programme *Investigating the President* aired on the night of Clinton's 'State of the Union' address on 26 January when they reported that Iraqi TV were showing *Wag the Dog*.

The capacity of Saddam to outsmart the USA and remain seemingly strengthened continued beyond Clinton's period in office. The catastrophe of September 11, 2001, however, transformed the already hawkish presidency of Bush Jnr into a 'War Against Terrorism' and at least within the USA afforded him sufficient political support to continue the military campaign against Saddam which his father had begun over a decade earlier. And yet, within the US and UK media, visual representations of Saddam had changed little, the images appeared to portray the ghost that Bush Snr had left in Baghdad in 1991. What had changed was a failing *belief* in the images standing for a madman who threatened the world. For example, the following is an excerpt from the *Donahue Show* broadcast in the period leading up to the Iraq War, involving a discussion between the host and a Republican Congressman:

[Video of **George Bush Senior** on Saddam:] The story of two young kids passing out leaflets. Iraqi troops rounded up their parents and made them watch while those two kids were shot to death, executed before their eyes. Hitler, revisited.

Donahue: This is a 12-year campaign to demonize Saddam Hussein. And he's still – we're still watching him fire that gun with that goofy hat.

Hunter: You left a few things out there. Since that speech by George Bush [Senior], the guy has killed his own son-in-laws. And he's killed over 100,000 people in his own country, the Kurdish people, 100,000 deaths. It's not something to sniff at. (*MSNBC,* Donahue Show, *4 September 2002*)

The image that Donahue refers to is a stock picture of Saddam firing a rifle into the air, which, depicting the Iraqi President as a solitary figure with a gun, is perhaps an unusual scene, but one that can be read as both 'madman' and 'menace'. But it is this image that Donahue uses to construct Saddam as a comical (and thus a harmless) figure, in contrast to the demonizing rhetoric of Bush Senior and the extension of this line by the Republican, Hunter. In effect, Donahue is asking 'What do have we to fear from such a figure?' The media in this way represent the world through visual stock images and then treat that world as if it were a reality. In the extract above we see a conflict between the common mediated visual images of Saddam (with 'goofy' hat), the widely-reported and mimicked demonic representations ('Hitler, revisited'), and some attempt at a simplistic numerical quantification of his 'evil' in terms of the deaths attributable to him. (The latter is standard fare in the electronic and print media where numbers (of deaths, casualties, demonstrators, etc.) instantly signify an event's status as news and the attention likely to be afforded it, and later as a template of similar or related news stories.) The result is a struggle played out on the talk shows over what has become a popular history of Saddam which cumulatively strengthened perceptions of his position far beyond his intentions and capabilities. The Hitler analogy was unsubstantiated, for as part of Saddam's utter demonization in the 1990s it became almost impossible for him to live up to such expectations. These, consequently, collapsed with the Iraq War which ushered in a new mediated Saddam – simply one that was no longer even 'there'.

SEARCHING FOR SADDAM

The US and UK invasion of Iraq in 2003 meant that the principal subject of their demonization of the previous decade was doomed. Once it became apparent that Saddam was not going to use chemical weapons (or did not even have such weapons for use) against the forces advancing against him, the demon was in effect extinguished. In these circumstances of the collapse of the metaphorical target in the present and future, some of the media resorted to assembling pre-emptive biographies (those that more usually *follow* in the wake of the death of a celebrity or figure of notoriety). On 12 April, for example, the *Daily Mirror* ran a three-page feature with the headline 'SADDAM HUSSEIN, DICTATOR, 1937–200? – A Life of Evil'. This charts the career of someone who 'first learnt the power of terror' (p. 8) as a six-year-old and traces in explicit and gruesome detail his rise and reign as dictator of Iraq, through to speculation on how he would be remembered, notably 'as blood-stained, power-crazed peasant like Stalin' (p. 9). The Hitler analogy is also prominent as a byline running across pages 8 and 9: 'RAISED BY A NAZI SYMPATHISER, TYRANT WHO MURDERED THOUSANDS'.

The extent and the effect of these representations of Saddam, however, were mediated by precisely a loss of faith in this discourse. The

Iraqi Information Minister, Mohammed Saeed al-Sahaf, for example, became the daily media face of the regime during the war. His utterances broadcast live to global audiences at daily briefings became increasingly colourful and incredible as the Americans advanced on Baghdad. Dubbed 'Comical Ali' overseeing his 'Ministry of Fun' in the West, he clearly enjoyed his performances although he appeared to share some of the delusions of his leader. Even when CNN and most global news networks were carrying extraordinary live pictures of Iraqi troops fleeing along the banks of the Tigris river, al-Sahaf, from a vantage point on the roof of Baghdad's Palestine Hotel, declared: 'Baghdad is safe. The battle is still going on. Their infidels are committing suicide by the hundreds on the gates of Baghdad . . . As our leader Saddam Hussein said, "God is grilling their stomachs in hell"' (*Guardian*, 8 April 2003, p. 8). Wearing Ba'ath Party uniform and black beret he inevitable conveyed something of Saddam about him, and yet despite (and because of) his rhetoric he appeared the antithesis of evil.

A tongue-in-cheek discourse on Saddam even emerged in some of the American media. As noted earlier in Chapter 3, the embedded and gung-ho Oliver North refers to Saddam as the '*Imelda Marcos* of grenades' which met with great approval from the TV anchor: 'Ollie, thank you so much. The *Imelda Marcos* of grenades – what a line!' (Fox News, 12 April 2003). The Iraqi President was fast becoming a figure of fun who was also playing games with the Americans as he managed to evade capture during the war. Saddam's ability to do precisely this was enhanced considerably with the emergence of the Arab satellite TV stations, who, as with videotapes of the much sought-after Osama bin Laden, provided an outlet for Saddam's continued media presence long after his regime had fallen.

The Western media that had helped to build the indefatigable evil persona of Saddam increasingly needed to find some closure in an image that could match those of his reign that was now jaded by history. The symbolic end came on 9 April in the form of the toppling of a ten-metre cast-iron statue in Paradise Square, Baghdad. A number of Iraqis had failed to make much of an impression with a sledgehammer on this towering structure when some US marines intervened with some cable and an armoured personnel carrier.

The images beamed live to a global audience and re-mediated across front pages around the world the following day appeared to signify the end of the man as well as the regime. However, on 18 April Abu Dhabi TV broadcast footage of Saddam dressed in familiar Ba'ath uniform and beret saluting a cheering crowd which it claimed was taken in Baghdad on the same day the statue (and capital) fell, and only some ten miles away. The remediation of these images in the West was part of a developing trend in Saddam's 'extended' presence, beyond the symbolic and declared end of the war, facilitated by the new Arab media players in the region wired into global news networks. However, a problem created by Saddam himself in his 'employment' of numerous body doubles is the doubt this inevitably cast over such recorded images. Images taken from this 'appearance' broadcast on Abu Dhabi TV filled newspaper front pages on 19 April. The *Guardian*, for example, treated the pictures with some scepticism, describing three reproductions across its front page as depicting 'a man said to be Saddam Hussein' (19 April 2003, p. 1).

Saddam's symbolic fall in the destruction of the statues, paintings and posters of him that dominated the public environment of Baghdad did not last for long. A 'new' Saddam was cast in the shadows of the disorder which came about with the end of the Iraq War, for he acquired greater mythical status through his disappearance. Given the failed demonizing rhetoric, ridicule appeared the last resort in an attempt to humiliate him. One news report even claimed that the US Army in Tikrit planned to put pictures up of Saddam's face superimposed on the bodies of various celebrities and film stars. These included Zsa Zsa Gabor, Elvis Presley and Billy Idol. A *Guardian* front page story was accompanied by the reproduction of a large manipulated photograph showing Saddam as Veronica Lake taken from the website www.worth1000.com (18 August 2003, p. 1). The article by Jamie Wilson entitled 'Fancy That? US Unveils New Secret Weapon' quotes Lieutenant-Colonel Steve Russell as saying: 'Most of the locals love 'em and they'll be laughing. But the bad guys are going to be upset, which will just make it easier for us to know who they are.' Perhaps these types of stories, not to mention the rise of 'Comical Ali', at least provided some light relief over a period of time when there was seemingly endless news on the Iraq War. What they also signify, however, is a barely concealed frustration, on the part of the USA particularly, of the irresolution of a war in which the principal enemy continued to find recognition on the world stage, even in spoof images.

The huge investment by the forces of the UK and USA (and cost in dead and injured) in prosecuting the Iraq War seemed to spiral out of control in the so-called 'post-war' period. At the same time a fresh media war erupted, particularly in the UK, where the fundamental justification for deposing Saddam of depriving him of 'his' WMDs were picked over (notably through the Hutton Inquiry into the suicide of a leading government advisor on WMDs, David Kelly). The war was simply harder to justify to an already sceptical British public under circumstances in which its main target had escaped. Max Hastings' reaction to the response by the USA and the UK as Saddam continued to evade them that the Iraq War was 'never personal', is that this is 'disingenuous':

> Since both Mr Blair and Mr Bush have compared Saddam with Hitler, it is fair to ask them what history would have thought, if the Fuhrer had enjoyed a comfortable retirement in Switzerland until his natural span expired some time around 1970.
>
> Before they can declare victory in their own terms, the allies need Saddam in their hands, alive or dead, just as they needed Osama bin Laden to claim decisive success in Afghanistan. Symbols matter. (*Daily Mail*, 16 April 2003, 'We're Still a Long Way From "Victory", Prime Minister', p. 20).

Saddam had become so iconic an enemy of the West that he, in the end, constituted a global presence over many years considerably disproportionate to the one he deserved and the one he would have achieved had he not been afforded such attention. Both reviled and ridiculed, the mediated images – stock images – enabled him to inhabit a considerable chunk of popular history.

And yet Saddam's capture on 14 December 2003 did not quite deliver the symbolic victory sought by Bush and Blair. For, unlike Uday and Qusay (who both died fighting) the image of Saddam in Western hands did not live up to his own rhetoric as amplified by American governments and their media. That the humiliation of Saddam was the greatest conceivable signification of 'victory' does not detract from the fraudulent nature of the image-driven media that misrepresented the former Iraqi ruler's global ambitions in the first place.

Chapter 6

The collapse of memory

SHARED VISIONS

The Gulf Wars of 1991 and 2003 bridge a historical gap of considerable change in media–military relations, in technological 'advances' in the waging and reporting of war, and consequently, in perceptions of security. Increasingly, the actions of war have entered publics' consciousness via television (and other media) at or close to their inception, changing forever the nature of collective and global understanding of events from distant battlefields. The cause, nature and outcomes of these wars have become increasingly contested through a media that has become synonymous with them. In this way our memory of warfare is entangled with a media that has transformed perceptions of conflict. On warfare, Paul Virilio, for example, argues,

> *the history of battle is primarily the history of radically changing fields of perception.* In other words, war consists not so much in scoring territorial, economic or other material victories as in appropriating the 'immateriality' of perceptual fields. (*1989: 7, original emphasis*)

Our 'perceptual fields' of recent conflicts have been re-visioned by the military, through the media; we have been afforded previously unimagined perspectives on warfare. On the one hand, technology has facilitated views and targets of the enemy from greater (and thus safer) distances, through satellite imaging and so-called 'smart' weaponry, whereas on the other, nightscape-aided equipment has enabled a greater proximity. The media offer similarly paradoxical perspectives. Talking heads comment endlessly on pictures from missile nose-cone and 'fixed' camera positions whilst embedded journalists have established a proximity at least to the troops, if not to their enemies.

It is not simply that those in the West embarking upon military action have become more strategic and involved in their management of the media, but that there has developed a mass news culture of war – a business in conflict. Coverage of the Gulf Wars has contributed significantly to the profile of particular news networks, with CNN feeding off its 1991 success for many years, and Fox News delivering its niche brand of gung-ho reporting to receptive US audiences in 2003. This period of the fragmentation of audiences and huge growth in news providers also coincides with a critical juncture in the intersection between the military and the media. As the output of the media has expanded with reality television formats driving swathes into schedules, news programming has had to provide literally a 'show' that is both live and intense in keeping with the dramatic form of the medium.

Audiences and correspondents both distanced in 1991 were seemingly brought closer to the zone of conflict over Iraq in 2003. News workers were embedded with the military on an unprecedented scale, enabling the documenting of the minutiae of the war as the distance between reporter and subject was erased. The ensuing simultaneous mass exposure of numerous pieces of the unfolding US and UK advance into Iraq, however, provided a somewhat schizophrenic picture. The closer the view and the more intensive the reporting, the more fractious the war appeared to become.

Embedded correspondents and their cameramen were often positioned with troops but at a (relatively safe) distance from engagement with the enemy. Television often looked out onto an expanse where movement and action was unfolding at some distance. The fact that the embeds could describe what they saw as eyewitnesses actually negated the need to show what could not be seen or could not be shown. Each embed functioned to provide signs of the war through the personalizing of their report (often exclusive to a particular battalion or regiment) – it was the only view in town. This kind of privileged reporting conveyed an authenticity and, when live, an immediacy that provided compulsive viewing. The standard fare of pool footage and recorded reports compiled from news agencies that produce picture clusters and dominate much television reporting was at times replaced by hundreds of truly unique perspectives.

On 23 March 2003, for example, Kerry Sanders, embedded with the 2nd Battalion, 8th Marines and reporting live for MSNBC, was crouched in the sand in Southern Iraq in flak jacket and goggles pulled up over a helmet so big that it obscured his eyes. Next to him, taking up half of the frame, lay a marine on his stomach seemingly oblivious to the reporting occurring right next to him with his gun pointed out over a ridge over an expanse of open ground. The shot is in bright daylight with a small plume of black smoke rising in the far distance. Sanders illustrates the advances of American divisions ahead of him in and around the city of An Nasiriya by drawing with his fingers in the sand a somewhat crude sketch of key points and the location and movement of companies of marines. His close proximity to the marine suggests a familiarity, almost as though Sanders is where he is for his own protection. Although the viewpoint of the embed is shared with that of the marine, their position is nonetheless one of relative safety, and Sanders' commentary is mostly limited to describing what he can see and the fact that he has been advised to stay where he is:

> **Anchor:** You get some sense of about how long you gonna be stuck in that position crouched down waiting to move?
>
> **Sanders:** Well we're crouched down quite frankly and you can see up there in the back that there's actually some people standing. We've been advised the best thing to do is to crouch down only because off there in the distance – er – there are some civilians and that those civilians could pose a threat because they may not be civilians they may be folks who are just Iraqi soldiers who are not in uniform. So we're staying down quite frankly just for the – er for our safety. You can see up there though up on the ridegeline some of the – er – some of the marines are taking positions where down there others are up and they're digging in. I even see one sort of adjusting his flak jacket because it's awfully hot out here. So that's the – the – situation out here. I mean these persons taking their – er – position on their own advice I guess you could say. (*MSNBC, live, 23 March 2003*)

The perspective afforded MSNBC viewers, however, is that of the eyeline of the invader. Sanders not only shares the TV frame with a marine but as with many of the embeds frequently refers to 'we', constructing the presence and actions of the 2nd Battalion as synonymous with his own. In this way it is not difficult to see how a shared vantage point is conflated with a shared perspective on the war and with the declared objectives of the marines on the road to Baghdad. By the removal of the distance between the media and the military, viewers are presented with a force seemingly unified in vision and in purpose. There seems very limited scope for critical reporting in these circumstances, with little 'time out' for embedded correspondents or opportunity to be 'off message'. The reporting of the 2003 Iraq War can thus be characterized as reporting of a highly *dependent* media, with true *in*dependent reporting limited to some notable journalists in the press, as I have shown in relation to the work of Robert Fisk, for example.

The restricted freedom of movement imposed on the embeds inevitably compromised their independence – yet this was the only (relatively) safe system of reporting the war available to many of them (and it was certainly not made available to all). Meanwhile, other correspondents in Iraq put themselves in greater danger and provided very different snapshots of the war. This included telling the story of when they themselves became a target.

EYEWITNESS IN THE LINE OF FIRE

One of the so-called 'friendly fire' incidents to make headline news in Britain was a single US missile attack on 6 April 2003 on a convoy of vehicles that included Americans, Kurds, and British newsworkers in southern Iraq. The BBC's World Affairs Editor John Simpson was caught up in this incident which killed at least eighteen (including his team's translator Kamaran Abdurazaq Muhammed) and wounded 45. The story was carried on a number of British newspaper front pages the next day, many with an accompanying frame grabbed from footage with blood visible on the camera lens.

Simpson returned to the scene only two days later to recount his experiences and record these for a programme for BBC News 24. He narrates his account of the attack whilst walking over and surveying the area that includes ground still stained by the blood of his interpreter. This is interspersed with footage depicting the chaotic scenes immediately after the missile struck, with white marked 'TV' and other vehicles ablaze amidst black smoke and the injured being hastily carried to safety. Simpson recalls the report he made by satellite phone and compares this with his reflections since, attempting to adjudge whether his remarks in his report (which were also printed in the British press) were appropriate:

I took the phone I started to do a broadcast to London. I remember – of course we were very hyped up and just full of adrenalin and excitement and horror and fear. I remember saying 'this is like a vision of hell' and I thought afterwards that's just silly kind of journalist language. But when I saw the *pictures* again and I thought about the experience and I thought about the man burning to death and I thought about our poor translator dying of blood loss there and the smoke and the flames and the noise and the mortars and the rockets and everything going off, I – well I think I wasn't really that far wrong, I think it was a vision of hell. (*Simpson's World, BBC News 24, 12 April 2003 (recorded 8 April 2003), spoken emphasis*)

The US friendly fire incident is an example of not just the fragmented nature of warfare itself, often being fought simultaneously in different places, but with reporters being similarly scattered over the battlefield it also provides an example of how audiences learn of events as a series of disconnected snapshots. Relative to the progress of the war the piece of land where the missile hit was insignificant, as Simpson makes clear in his report: 'So this is the scene, a little crossroads I don't think marked on maps really. In a village whose name nobody knows, on an approach to a town that nobody has heard of and not very many people care about' (ibid.). What makes the story significant as news is that it involves the Americans firing on their own side. Of even greater news value, however, is that members of the media were hit and thus the subject of the story could also report the story.

Simpson's report for News 24 is sombre in tone and he is still partially deaf from his experience of two days earlier. His retelling of the story is interesting because he compares his live reporting of the aftermath of the missile strike with his subsequent reflections. He challenges his own eyewitness account and the appropriateness of his description of the scene resembling 'a vision of hell'. However, it is not his own memory of the event that is sufficient for him, for given the intense nature and shock of the experience, he feels he may have become 'carried away' in the moment of reporting. The reliability of eyewitness accounts, as with all accounts based upon human memory, should be treated with some caution. As Gergen (2000: 163), for example, argues: 'As research on eyewitness testimony demonstrates, reports of the past are not like photographs, fixed and final. Rather, they are continuously in motion, altered with new information and experience.' Yet Simpson reflects on his own memory of the missile attack upon seeing the footage recorded by his cameraman. This appears to verify his original reported description as he matches up the two representations. And this is precisely the approach of the programme in using flashbacks taken from film footage of the event to support Simpson's report.

The *Simpson's World* programme produces a very powerful and convincing documentation of the events of the 6 April through combining eyewitness testimony (as narration), film taken from the time, and the fact that the retelling of the story occurs in the *place* of the story (I examined the significance of place in memory in Chapter 4). As a journalist and subject his personal experience lends an authenticity to this account as narrator. The same effect is provided by a colleague who also contributes. In respect of the combination of these elements, it is difficult to conceive of a stronger form of remembering. Note though how Simpson is more confident in his subsequent viewing of the visual images than from his own reporting of the event two days earlier. This raises a more interesting question in terms of how his memory of this incident will change or remain the same in future times.

Simpson's reflections represent a microcosm of how the media routinely treat past events. Recorded visual images maintain a certain representation of events over time, although interpretations and meanings evoked by those images may be transformed. What the media do provide are visual scripts against which past events can be 'checked', perhaps precisely in the light of new information about them. For example, the symbolic end of Saddam in the toppling of his statue in Paradise Square, Baghdad, has since been re-interpreted as a staged and 'false' end to the Iraq War by numerous commentators. The point is that when the media are so significant in forging the memory of an event they can powerfully unravel this memory as easily as they can sustain it.

The old cliché that if the media do not report an event as news than it 'does not happen' can be extended to journalists themselves: the greater their personal involvement and in some ways 'insight' into a story, the more reportable the story becomes. In the Iraq War, embedded and other journalists frequently displaced eyewitnesses (the traditional sources of news reports), with themselves as central narrators events. In these circumstances, correspondents getting the story increasingly can be perceived as *making* the story. This trend is notable in a number of BBC television *Panorama* documentaries on the Iraq War in which a number of 'experts' on warfare were gathered in a studio to debate the pros and cons of the conflict and comment on likely scenarios and outcomes. However, journalists increasingly appeared as experts themselves: after all, they were the eyewitnesses to war and could talk with authority on their experiences. Similarly, one of the first books published on the Iraq War was *The Battle for Iraq: BBC News Correspondents on the War Against Saddam and a New World Agenda* (2003). Putting aside issues of the branding and promotion of the role of BBC journalists, significant questions arise in terms of what *kind* of history will emerge of the Iraq War if the most extensive and authentic (e.g. eyewitness testimony) documentation is constituted on an extensive scale through the reports and diaries of journalists? In the production of multiple extensive eyewitness accounts through the embedded and other co-present reporting of war, have journalists become more influential arbiters of a history of such events? And do the scattered although authentic snapshots of the Iraq War constitute a coherent narrative of events that will be remembered by audiences who watched? These are some of the questions that are at the heart of the construction of new memory.

THE COLLAPSE OF MEMORY

Television news in particular contributes significantly to the resonance of events in new memory in later times. Central to this relationship is the attachment or otherwise from the original event by the person doing the remembering. Journalists as witnesses to as well as narrators of news events, if not 'historians' exactly, nonetheless have become principle conveyors of a mediated or televised past.

For audiences, however, it appears that not only is television key in the later remembering of news events, but it can become increasingly so over time. Ulric Neisser and Nicole Harsch, for example, from their research into recollections of the American space shuttle *Challenger* disaster (which was witnessed by vast audiences live on television in 1986) found that even very vivid memories can be mistaken. They examined the origin and endurance of so-called 'flashbulb memories' (Brown and Kulik, 1977[42]), which are so confidently recalled it is as though they are reproduced directly from the witnessing of the 'original' event, including instances in which this was viewed on television. Neisser and Harsch (1992: 30) argue: 'Our data leave no doubt that vivid and confident flashbulb recollections can be mistaken. When this happens, the original memories seem to have disappeared entirely.' That is to say, the original experiencing of the news event is forgotten, or re-constructed in the light of subsequent viewings of the images repeated on television. So, for those subjects of this study who later came to believe they first witnessed the *Challenger* explosion on TV, television was key to the remembered event (ibid, 28).

A shift toward 'TV priority' that Neisser and Harsch show in their study of remembering suggests the centrality of the medium in establishing images of catastrophe and warfare in public consciousness through their repetition. Moreover, they argue that the watching of television is not so easily associated with a clear sequence of events or 'script' of before, during and after an event experienced personally, in order to aid in the viewer's reconstruction from their memory. For audiences, then, there occurs literally a *collapse* of memory that is founded upon the vicarious televisual experiencing of events, that is to say television as a medium of memory does not afford the same personal scripts and sequential narratives that are central to the locating of our experiences in the past, i.e. the memory is reduced to 'we saw it on TV'. Instead, television news subverts, replaces, rewinds and mixes times and images into its own continuously moving narrative in the present that literally samples and revives some past events at the expense of others.

Consider, for example, how difficult it is to locate many of the media representations of Saddam Hussein in a definitive past context. As I have shown, many of the simplistic and stock images of Saddam tend to 'float free' of the original time and place of their recording. Television detaches the past from the present in this way as much as it connects it through templates. Yet, does the repetitious television environment really diminish engagement and memory through its treatment of more graphic images, i.e. those that by their very shocking nature might be regarded as more memorable?

In 2003 Susan Sontag claimed to be less certain about her earlier argument that the repeated exposure to photographs have a diminishing impact on the conscience of the viewer. As noted in Chapter 2, Sontag argues that television as the principal medium of news has been seen to weaken attention and sympathy in images of war and atrocity by habituating them. Or, at least that the nature of the medium induces a certain cynicism amongst critics: 'Flooded with images of the sort that once used to shock and arouse indignation, we are losing our capacity to react. Compassion, stretched to its limits, is going numb. So runs the familiar diagnosis' (2003: 108). The time between Sontag's two works in question, *On Photography* (1977) and *Regarding the Pain of Others* (2003), is marked by atrocities unthinkable in a late twentieth-century world, in Bosnia, Rwanda and Yugoslavia, for example, as well as being a period of exponential growth in news media that documented the horrors of genocide and 'ethnic cleansing'. However, Sontag asks if, amongst the saturation of images and the greater reach of news, one can still be mobilized into opposing a war by an image or a set of images. Her answer is that this depends: 'Partly it is a question of the length of time one is obliged to look, to feel' (2003: 122). So, television may not obligate much responsibility either through the necessarily limited periods of exposure to images, or, equally, through repeated transient glimpses of them. In this way, as Jerry Kuehl (1988: 446) argues, television is a medium that 'offers its audience virtually no time for reflection'.

Of course, much of Sontag's work refers to the images of atrocity that did (and do) appear on our television screens, which was not the case in the coverage of the wars fought mostly by the USA against Iraq in 1991 and 2003. Although I have a living memory of the TV coverage of the Gulf War, the image from this conflict that I remember most vividly is a much more recently published photograph of an American bulldozer and soldiers burying the Iraqi dead on the road to Basra. This was reproduced in black-and-white in the *Guardian's* 'Unseen Gulf War' *G2* supplement of 14 February 2003.

On the notorious 'Highway of Death' the mystery as to the absence of the bodies of Iraqis appearing in the media along with the twisted wreckage of their vehicles (with the key exception of the Jarecke photograph) was explained by their rapid burial by the Americans. Sloyan (2003), for example, reports:

> Thousands of Iraqi soldiers, some of them firing their weapons from first world war-style trenches, had been buried by ploughs mounted on Abrams tanks. The tanks had flanked the lines so that tons of sand from the plough spoil had funnelled into the trenches. Just behind the tanks, straddling the trench line, came Bradleys pumping machine-gun bullets into Iraqi troops.

This narrative and other similarly shocking descriptions (for example, see John Pilger[43]), however, are not the primary reason for the image of this atrocity remaining vividly in my memory. The photograph in the *Guardian* taken by Peter Turnley reminded me of another image: a black-and white photograph of the burial of the dead at the Bergen-Belsen Nazi concentration camp. This depicts a man with a scarf over his nose and mouth driving a tractor pushing along towards the camera an entanglement of the emaciated limbs and torsos of those who had not survived to be liberated. Bulldozers were used to bury the mass of bodies in an attempt to prevent the spread of disease. This image I recall from visiting the Holocaust Exhibition in the Imperial War Museum, London. The photograph has been reproduced and enlarged so that it fills a space from the floor to the ceiling and thus commands a significant presence in the Exhibition.

My memory of the Turnley photograph is thus based on recognition – an individual template – as much as its shocking nature. Both images, one in a newspaper, and particularly the one in the Holocaust Exhibition, are simply easier to place, to locate as part of a 'personal script', than even more harrowing images I have seen on television. The static image in this way can be seen as the very antithesis of the televisual image in its resonance in memory, for the latter closes down time and space for reflection. So, as Sontag observes, even shocking or what she terms 'ultimate' images (i.e. of the Holocaust) 'weigh differently' when seen in different contexts, e.g. the museum, gallery catalogue, newsprint or television (2003: 119–20).

As new and more immediate ways are found to document wars and other catastrophes, the media accumulate ever more images that contribute to a collapse of memory. Television delivers mostly a memory of convenience (disturbing images that do not last long on the screen, or better still, wars with injury and death glossed over). The Gulf Wars, as I have shown, cast uneasy historical shadows in the suspicion of what remains unseen and unknown. The military rather than the media have effectively appropriated technological advances in news gathering and reporting. The result is a paradox between a sanitized version of wars that we in the West fight and watch and remember, and those of other nations whose loss of life is seen and forgotten, and, more often, not seen and not remembered.

Notes

1 The concentration of ownership and control of media organizations has skewed a global memory of world events around Western news values. However, the same technologies that enabled this dominant version of world events to be reflected globally are now being used to challenge such views, with the recent rise in satellite news networks in the Arab World, for example.

2 Alastair Cooke, 'The anxiety of war', *Letter From America*, 31 March 2003 at http://news.bbc.co.uk/1/hi/world/letter_from_america/2902237.stm, accessed 4 April 2003.

3 This concept was used in conversation by Deirdre Boden, London, 2000. See also Andrew Hoskins, 'Flashframes of History: American Televisual Memories' in Beck, John and Holloway, David (eds) (forthcoming) *American Visual Cultures*, London: Continuum.

4 See Deborah Esch (1999) 'No time like the present' at http://www.pum.umontreal.ca/revues/surfaces/vol3/esch.html (accessed 23 March 2003).

5 Paul Gilroy explores the relationship between 'tradition, modernity, temporality and social memory' in his examination of *The Black Atlantic*. He critiques the Africentrism understanding of 'tradition' as constant repetition, as opposed to being employed as a spur to transformation.

6 This is the actual time of the news programme after commercials are excluded, see Todd Gitlin, 1980: 265.

7 Stock images are those most often re-selected by news and picture editors (in print as well as television) to provide an immediate visual framing of a story based upon previous media depictions of relevant characters and events. I explore this phenomenon in Chapter 5 in relation to media representations of Saddam Hussein.

8 This term was used in conversation by Deirdre Boden, London, 2000. See also the comparison mark with so-called 'flashbulb' memories in Chapter 6.

9 *Vietnam: the Camera at War*, BBC2, broadcast during 1999.

10 Ibid.

11 For example, the Holocaust Exhibition at the Imperial War Museum, London, displays some images of perpetrators and victims of the Holocaust that are not already widely received in popular history alongside those that are (interview with Victoria Cook, Assistant Curator, Holocaust Exhibition, IWM, 27 March 2003).

12 Sontag was interviewed by Geoffrey Movius of the *Boston Review* online at http://bostonreview.mit.edu/BR01.1/sontag.html (accessed 10 December 2002).

13 However, images grabbed from television news and re-mediated in print today sometimes carry signs of the increased complexity of their sourcing and presentation. See the *Mirror* extract in Figure 3, for example. Although showing only a portion of the TV view of a POW from 1991 and 2003, this reveals cumulative signs of the latter's broadcast on Iraqi TV, Al Jazeera and the British-based Sky News channel.

14 For example, see the *The Times, Guardian, Sun, Mirror, Daily Express* and *Daily Mail*.

15 For a detailed analysis of the impact of the temporalities in the TV environment of GWI, see Hoskins, 2001a: 220–30.

16 *In Memoriam: New York City*, Channel 4, broadcast 11 March 2002.

17 *People's Century* – 'Picture Power', broadcast 24 August 1998, BBC2. The series from which this quote is taken – the BBC's *People's Century* – is an attempt to provide a televisual view, or record, of history. In the programme, the original night-scope footage is re-matched with a piece of the audio of Bernard Shaw reporting from the al-Rashid Hotel, Baghdad.

18 The ABC cameraman Fabrice Moussu was widely acclaimed for delivering the first film footage of the war and himself appeared in front of the camera to talk about his role, e.g. on the French television news programme *20 Hueres*, TF1, 22 January 1991.

19 Nichol's article provides a personal angle on the experience of the POWs and he claims that these images will not serve Iraqi propaganda, as does an article below on the same page, strangely juxtaposed with a view from the commentator Routledge who points out the hypocrisy of Americans who make this complaint, given the USA's own treatment of POWs elsewhere in the world. This is an example of the fine line the *Daily Mirror* took in opposing the Iraq War, but being seen to be supportive of UK servicemen and women in action in the Middle East.

20 I examine the history and the impact of this photograph in Chapter 5.

21 Johan Galtung and Mari Holmboe Ruge (1965) identify twelve (complementary) conditions for events to satisfy in order to become news and claim that there is a 'threshold value' for each type of story or event to reach in order for it to make the news, thus the phrase 'news value'.

22 I argue that the model of news values (derived from Galtung and Ruge, 1965 and their research into the coverage of three international crises in four Norwegian newspapers) still dominant in the teaching of media studies and journalism today is often employed uncritically and has limited application in explanations of today's TV news environments. See Andrew Hoskins (2002) and Hoskins (forthcoming).

23 Mark Lawson (2003a), Section 2, p. 17.

24 See also Helga Nowotny (1994), pp. 71–2.

25 As Michael Arlen (1982: 72) points out: 'CBS's Dave Schoumacher and his Australian cameraman and his Vietnamese sound man, with their seventy pounds of equipment, comprised a troika that was neither mobile nor particularly self-effacing.'

26 Jean Baudrillard (1988: 7) argues: 'Speed creates a space of initiation, which may be lethal; its only rule is to leave no trace behind. Triumph of forgetting over memory, an uncultivated, amnesiac intoxication. The superficiality and reversibility of a pure object in the pure geometry of the desert.'

27 This footage provoked considerable controversy beyond its content when allegations that this was ten-year-old CNN video took hold of message boards and various sites across the internet. Eventually, CNN took the unusual step of issuing a statement to

officially deny the allegation and to clarify the source of the footage. See http://www. cnn.com/2001/US/09/20/cnn.statement/index.html (accessed 22 September 2001).

28 See John Glover (2003).

29 Nik Gowing has been developing his thesis for several years on the impact of real-time television news on politicians and policy, see for example Gowing (1994).

30 See Robert Fisk, 'Does Tony Have Any Idea What the Flies are Like that Feed Off the Dead?', *Independent*, 26 April 2003, p. 17.

31 Kahn (1992) traces the historical shortening of the 'body lag' from World War I through to the 1991 Gulf War.

32 Unidentified AP editor cited in Jacqueline E. Sharkey (2003), p. 22.

33 John Taylor provides a detailed analysis of the original publication context, and reading of the Jarecke image in the *Guardian* and *Observer* of 1991, in *Body Horror: Photojournalism, Catastrophe and War*, pp. 167, 181–3, in which this photograph is also reproduced.

34 Philip M. Taylor (1995) 'War and the Media' at http://www.leeds.ac.uk/ics/arts-pt2.htm (accessed 10 July 2002).

35 Martin Bell interviewed on *Channel 4 News*.

36 The work of freelance journalists in particular has attracted greater attention over the past decade or so. For example, the annual Rory Peck Awards were named after a freelance cameraman killed in Moscow in 1993 and established to acknowledge and increase awareness of the work of freelance broadcast journalists.

37 Brian Walden, *Walden on Villains*, BBC2 series, in 1998.

38 Ibid.

39 The transparency of the visual iconic image of war not only seduces the media. The Saddam–Lockwood image, for example, is reproduced in a television screen twelve times on the cover of Cumings (1992) *War and Television*, and yet does not receive a mention in the book itself.

40 See Hoskins (2001b: 337–9) for analysis of the US television use of these images.

41 Fouad Ajami uses this expression in describing Bush's concerns that this is precisely how Saddam is viewed in the region and hence Bush's need for the Hitler comparison and the assembling of a wide Coalition (speaking on CBS *Evening News*, 1 November 1990).

42 Brown and Kulik (1977) asked respondents in 1975 about their memories of the 1963 assassination of President John F. Kennedy, and found that many attributed great significance to the context in which they learned of the news (i.e. where they were and what they were doing) even if this was mis-remembered.

43 Pilger (2000) 'Iraq: Paying the Price', article at http://pilger.carlton.com/iraq/articles/19182 (accessed 10 December 2002).

References

BOOKS AND JOURNAL ARTICLES

Abercrombie, Nicholas and Longhurst, Brian (1998) *Audiences – A Sociological Theory of Performance and Imagination*, London: Sage.

Adam, Barbara (1990) *Time and Social Theory*, Cambridge: Polity Press.

Allan, Stuart (1999) *News Culture*, Buckingham: Open University Press.

Arcaya, Jose M. (1992) 'Why is Time not Included in Modern Theories of Memory?', *Time and Society*, 1, 301–14.

Arlen, Michael J. (1969) *Living Room War*, New York: The Viking Press.

Arlen, Michael J. (1982) 'The Falklands, Vietnam, and Our Collective Memory', *The New Yorker*, 16 August, pp. 70–5.

Baudrillard, Jean (1988) *America* (trans. Christ Turner), London: Verso.

Baudrillard, Jean (1995 [1991]) *The Gulf War Did Not Take Place* (trans. Paul Patton), Sydney: Power Publications.

Baudrillard, Jean (1994) *The Illusion of the End*, Cambridge: Polity Press.

Bell, Allan (1998) 'The Discourse Structure of News Stories' in Bell, Allan and Garrett, Peter (eds) *Approaches to Media Discourse*, Oxford: Blackwell Publishers, pp. 64–104.

Bell, Martin (1998) 'The Journalism of Attachment' in Kieran, Matthew (ed.) *Media Ethics*, London: Routledge, pp. 15–22.

Boden, Deirdre and Hoskins, Andrew (1995) 'Time, Space and Television'. Unpublished paper presented at 2nd Theory, Culture & Society Conference, 'Culture and Identity: City, Nation, World', Berlin, 11 August 1995.

Bolter, Jay David and Grusin, Richard (1999) *Remediation: Understanding New Media*, London: The MIT Press.

Braestrup, Peter (1983/1977) *Big Story: How the American Press and Television Reported and Interpreted the Crisis of Tet 1968 in Vietnam and Washington* (abridged edition), New Haven: Yale University Press.

Brown, Roger and Kulik, James (1977) 'Flashbulb Memories', *Cognition*, 5, 73–99.

Caldwell, John Thornton (1995) *Televisuality – Style, Crisis, and Authority in American Television*, New Brunswick: Rutgers University Press.

Cubitt, Sean (1991) *Timeshift – On Video Culture*, London: Routledge.

Cumings, Bruce (1992) *War and Television*, London: Verso.

Denton, Robert E., Jr (ed.) (1993) *The Media and the Persian Gulf War*, London: Praeger Publishers.

Doane, Mary Ann (1990) 'Information, Crisis, Catastrophe' in Mellencamp, Patricia (ed.) *Logics of Television: Essays in Cultural Criticism*, London: BFI, pp. 222–39.

Feuer, Jane (1983) 'The Concept of Live Television: Ontology as Ideology' in Kaplan, Ann E. (ed.) (1983) *Regarding Television, Critical Approaches – An Anthology*, Los Angeles: University Publications of America, pp. 12–22.

Galtung, Johan and Ruge, Mari Holmboe (1965), 'The Structure of Foreign News: The Presentation of the Congo, Cuba, and Cyprus Crises in Four Norwegian Newspapers', *Journal of Peace Research*, 2(1), 64–91.

Garrett, Laura (1991) 'What We Saw, What We Learned', *Columbia Journalism Review*, 30(1), 32.

Gergen, Kenneth J. (2000) *The Saturated Self: Dilemmas of Identity in Contemporary Life*, New York: Basic Books.

Gillespie, Marie (2002) Audience Research Study, 'After September 11: TV News and Transnational Audiences' Project (see also www.afterseptember11.tv).

Gilroy, Paul (1993) *The Black Atlantic – Modernity and Double Consciousness*, London: Verso.

Gitlin, Todd (1980) *The Whole World is Watching – Mass Media in the Making and Unmaking of the New Left*, London: University of California Press.

Gitlin, Todd (2001) *Media Unlimited: How the Torrent of Images and Sounds Overwhelms Our Lives*, New York: Metropolitan Books.

Glover, John (2003) 'Television Coverage of the War in Iraq', ITC Information Paper, 37/03.

Gowing, Nik (1994) 'Real-Time Television Coverage of Armed Conflicts and Diplomatic Crises: Does it Pressure or Distort Foreign Policy Decisions?', Harvard University: The Joan Shorenstein Barone Centre on the Press, Politics and Public Policy, John F. Kennedy School of Government, Working Paper 94-1.

Grainge, Paul (2002) *Monochrome Memories: Nostalgia and Style in Retro America*, Westport, CT: Praeger.

Halbwachs, Maurice (1992/1952) *On Collective Memory* (trans. by Lewis A. Coser from *Les cadres sociaux de la mémoire* (1952) Paris: Presses Universitaires de France and from *La topographie légendaire des évangiles en terre sainte: Etude de mémoire collective* (1941) Paris: Presses Universitaires de France), London: The University of Chicago Press.

Hallin, Daniel C. (1986) *The Uncensored War: The Media and Vietnam*, New York: Oxford University Press.

Hargreaves, Ian and Thomas, James (2002) *New News, Old News*, London: ITC/BSC.

Hoskins, Andrew (2001a) 'Mediating Time: The Temporal Mix of Television', *Time & Society*, 10(2/3), 333–46.

Hoskins, Andrew (2001b) 'New Memory: Mediating History', *The Historical Journal of Film, Radio and Television*, 21(4), 191–211.

Hoskins, Andrew (2002) 'Goodbye News Values: New(s) Times in Media Studies', presented at the 4th Annual MeCCSA Conference, University of Reading, 18 December 2002.

Hoskins, Andrew (2004) 'Television and the Collapse of Memory', *Time and Society* 13(1), 109–27.

Hoskins, Andrew (forthcoming) *Television Discourse*, London: Arnold.

Kahn, Douglas (1992) 'Body Lags' in Peters, Nancy. J. (ed.) *War After War*, San Francisco, City Lights Books, pp. 43–6.

Kitzinger, Jenny (2000) 'Media Templates: Key Events and the (Re)construction of Meaning, *Media, Cultura and Society*, 22(1), 61–84.

Knightley, Phillip (2003) 'History or Bunkum?', *British Journalism Review*, 14(2), 7–14.

Kuehl, Jerry (1988) 'History on the Public Screen, II' in Rosenthal, Alan (ed.) *New Challenges for Documentary*, Berkeley: University of California Press, pp. 444–53.

Livingston, Steven (1997) 'Clarifying the CNN Effect: An Examination of Media Effects According to Type of Military Intervention', Research Paper R-18, The Joan Shorenstein Centre, Harvard University.

MacGregor, Brent (1997) *Live, Direct and Biased? Making Television News in the Satellite Age*, London: Arnold.

McLuhan, Marshall (1962) 'A Sheet' – 'The TV Image: One of Our Conquerors' in Molinaro, Matie *et al.* (eds) (1987) *Letters of Marshall McLuhan*, Oxford: Oxford University Press.

McLuhan, Marshall (1962, 1987) *The Gutenberg Galaxy – the Making of Typographic Man*, London: Routledge and Kegan Paul.

McLuhan, Marshall (1964) *Understanding Media – The Extensions of Man*, London: Routledge and Kegan Paul.

McLuhan, Marshall and Fiore, Quentin (2001/1968) *War and Peace in the Global Village*, Corte Madera: Gingko Press.

Marriott, Stephanie (1995) 'Intersubjectivity and Temporal Reference in Television Commentary', *Time and Society*, 4(3), 345–64.

Meyrowitz, Joshua (1985) *No Sense of Place*, Oxford: Oxford University Press.

Moeller, Susan D. (1999) *Compassion Fatigue: How the Media Sell Disease, Famine, War and Death*, London: Routledge.

Neisser, Ulric and Harsch, Nicole (1992) 'Phantom Flashbulbs: False Recollections of Hearing the News About Challenger' in Neisser, Elric (ed.) *Memory Observed. Remembering in Natural Contexts*, San Francisco: W.H. Freeman and Company.

Norman, Donald A. (1976) *Memory and Attention: An Introduction to Human Information Processing* (2nd edn), London: John Wiley and Sons.

Nowotny, Helga (1994) *Time – The Modern and Postmodern Experience*, Cambridge: Polity Press.

Postman, Neil (1987) *Amusing Ourselves to Death – Public Discourse in the Age of Show Business*, London: Methuen.

Puttnam, David (2003) 'News: You Want it Quick or Do You Want it Good?', *British Journalism Review*, 14(2), 50–7.

Reading, Anna (2002) *The Social Inheritance of the Holocaust: Gender, Culture and Memory*, Basingstoke: Palgrave Macmillan.

Robinson, Piers (2002) *The CNN Effect: The Myth of News, Foreign Policy and Intervention*, London: Routledge.

Rose, Steven (1993) *The Making of Memory: From Molecules to Mind*. London: Bantam Books.

Samuel, Raphael (1994) *Theatres of Memory, Volume 1: Past and Present in Contemporary Culture*, London: Verso.

Scarry, Elaine (1985) *The Body in Pain – The Making and Unmaking of the World*, Oxford: Oxford University Press.

Schudson, Michael (1987) 'When? Deadlines, Datelines, and History' in Schudson, Michael and Manoff, Robert Karl (eds) *Reading the News*, New York: Pantheon Books, pp. 79–108.

Schudson, Michael (1990) 'Ronald Reagan Misremembered' in Middleton, David and Edwards, Derek (eds) *Collective Remembering*, London: Sage, pp. 109–19.

Shandler, Jeffrey (1999) *While America Watches: Televising the Holocaust*, New York: Oxford University Press.

Shapiro, Michael J. (1997) *Violent Cartographies – Mapping Cultures of War*, London: University of Minnesota Press.

Sharkey, Jacqueline E. (2003) 'Airing Graphic Footage', *American Journalism Review*, May, p. 22.

Shaw, Donald L. and Martin, Shannon E. (1993) 'The Natural, and Inevitable Phases of War Reporting: Historical Shadows, New Communication in the Persian Gulf' in Denton, R. E. (ed.) *The Media and the Persian Gulf War*, Westport, CT: Praegar, pp. 43–70.

Sontag, Susan (1977) *On Photography*, London: Penguin.

Sontag, Susan (2003) *Regarding the Pain of Others*, New York: Farrar, Straus and Giroux.

Steiner, George (1991) *Real Presences*, Chicago: University of Chicago Press.

Sturken, Marita (1997) *Tangled Memories: The Vietnam War, the AIDS Epidemic, and the Politics of Remembering*, London: University of California Press.

Sturken, Marita (2002) 'Television Vectors and the Making of a Media Event: The Helicopter, The Freeway Chase, and National Memory' in Friedman, James (ed.) *Reality Squared: Televisual Discourse on the Real*, New Brunswick: Rutgers University Press, pp. 185–202.

Taylor, John (1998) *Body Horror: Photojournalism, Catastrophe and War*, Manchester: Manchester University Press.

Taylor, Philip M. (1998/1992) *War and the Media: Propaganda and Persuasion in the Gulf War* (2nd edn), Manchester: Manchester University Press.

Urry, John (1994) 'Time, Leisure and Social Identity', *Time and& Society*, 3(2), 131–49.

Urry, John (2002) *Sociology Beyond Societies: Mobilities for the Twenty-first Century*, London: Routledge.

Virilio, Paul (1989) *War and Cinema: The Logistics of Perception*, London: Verso.

Virilio, Paul (1994) *The Vision Machine*, London: British Film Institute.

Volkmer, Ingrid (1999) *News in the Global Sphere: A Study of CNN and its Impact on Global Communication*, Luton: University of Luton Press.

Wark, McKenzie (1994) *Virtual Geography – Living with Global Media Events*, Bloomington: Indiana University Press.

Zelizer, Barbie (1998) *Remembering to Forget: Holocaust Memory Through the Camera's Eye*, London: The University of Chicago Press.

PRINT MEDIA

Berger, John (1991) 'In the land of the deaf', *Guardian*, 2 March 1991.

Branigin, William (2003) 'A Gruesome Scene on Highway 9: 10 Dead After Vehicle Shelled at Checkpoint', *Washington Post*, 1 April 2003, p. A01.

Fisk, Robert (2003) 'Does Tony have any idea what the flies are like that feed off the dead'?, *The Independent on Sunday*, 26 January 2003, p. 21.

Fisk, Robert (2003) 'Is there some element in the US military that wants to take out journalists'? *Independent*, 9 April 2003.

Fisk, Robert (2003) 'Did the US murder these journalists'? *Independent*, 26 April 2003, p. 17.

Franchetti, Mark (2003) 'Mad Max Onslaught of the Marines', *The Sunday Times*, 23 March 2003.

Goodman, Walter (1990) 'Iraq's Leader Entertains "Guests", Not "Hostages"', *New York Times*, 24 August 1990, p. A11.
Guardian (14 February 2003) 'The Unseen Gulf War', *G2* Section.
Gowing, Nik (2002) 'Don't Get in Our Way', *Media Guardian*, 8 April 2002.
Hastings, Max (2003) 'We're still a long way from "victory", Prime Minister', *Daily Mail*, 16 April 2003, p. 20.
Herbert, Hugh (1991) 'Television: Damoclean Deficits, Rampant Recession and Some Unstoppably Brilliant Art. Virtual Unreality', *Guardian*, 30 December 1991.
Iannucci, Armando (2003) 'Shoot Now, Think Later', *Guardian*, 28 April 2003, p. 16.
Katz, Elihu (1991) 'Notes on Watching the War', *The Jerusalem Report*, 31 January 1991, p. 44.
Lawson, Mark (2003a) 'The Merits of Broadcasting Live', *Guardian,* 31 March 2003, Section 2, p. 17.
Lawson, Mark (2003b) 'Off to War with the Armchair Division', *Guardian*, 24 March 2003.
McCabe, Eamonn (1991) 'Dilemma of the grisly and the gratuitous', *A Guardian*, 4 March 1991.
Nichol, John (2003) 'Horrific, Inhuman, Exclusive: Ordeal Facing U.S. PoWs', Daily Mirror, 23 March 2003, p. 4.
Preston, Peter (2003) 'Censoring the Dead', *Guardian*, 14 April 2003
Raban, Jonathan (2003) 'The Greatest Gulf', *Guardian* 'Review', 19 April 2003, pp. 4–6.
Rosenberg, Howard (1990) 'Dan and Saddam Show: CBS' Prime-Time Coup', *Los Angeles Times*, 31 August 1990, p. F1.
Sloyan, Patrick J. (2003) Untitled article in 'The Unseen Gulf War', *Guardian*, 14 February, p. 14.
Swain, Gill (2003) 'A Life of Evil', *Daily Mirror*, 12 April 2003, pp. 7–9.
Swain, Jon (2002) 'Why the Reporter is the Last Bastion of Truth', *Observer*, 16 March 2003, p. 29.
Watt, Nicholas (2003) 'Baghdad is Safe, the Infidels are Committing Suicide', *Guardian*, 8 April 2003, p. 8.
Wilson, Jamie (2003) 'It Felt Like Being Back at School', *Media Guardian*, 7 April 2003, p. 5.
Wolff, Michael (2003) 'I Was Only Asking', *Media Guardian*, 14 April 2003, pp. 6–7.

BROADCAST MEDIA

Bell, Martin (2003) *Gash*, Channel 4, 28 April 2003.
In Memoriam: New York City, Channel 4, 11 March 2002.

INTERNET

CNN statement at: http://www.cnn.com/2001/US/09/20/cnn.statement/index.html (accessed 22 September 2001).
Cooke, Alastair (2003) 'The anxiety of war', *Letter From America*, 31 March 2003 at: http://news.bbc.co.uk/1/hi/world/letter_from_america/2902237.stm (accessed 4 April 2003).
Esch, Deborah (1999) 'No time like the present' at: http://www.pum.umontreal.ca/revues/surfaces/vol3/esch.html (accessed 23 March 2003).
Hinsliff, Gaby (2003) 'One Ali saved, but thousands more are suffering', 10 August 2003,

the   *Observer*,   at:
http://observer.guardian.co.uk/politics/story/0,6903,1015861,00.html (accessed 15
August 2003).
Pilger, John (2000) 'Iraq: Paying the Price' at: http://pilger.carlton.com/iraq/articles/
19182 (accessed 4 June 2002).
Sontag, Susan (1975) interviewed by Geoffrey Movius of the *Boston Review*, online at:
http://bostonreview.mit.edu/BR01.1/sontag.html (accessed 10 December 2002).
Taylor, Philip M. (1995) 'War and the Media' at: http://www.leeds.ac.uk/ics/arts-pt2.htm
(accessed 10 July 2002).

Index

Entries in bold refer to illustrations